NEW DIRECTIONS FOR MENTAL HEALTH SERVICES

H. Richard Lamb, *University of Southern California*
EDITOR-IN-CHIEF

Psychiatric Aspects of Violence: Issues in Prevention and Treatment

Carl C. Bell
Community Mental Health Council, Inc.
University of Illinois

EDITOR

Number 86, Summer 2000

JOSSEY-BASS
San Francisco

PSYCHIATRIC ASPECTS OF VIOLENCE: ISSUES IN PREVENTION AND TREATMENT
Carl C. Bell (ed.)
New Directions for Mental Health Services, no. 86
H. Richard Lamb, Editor-in-Chief

Microfilm copies of issues and articles are available in 16mm and 35mm, as well as microfiche in 105mm, through University Microfilms Inc., 300 North Zeeb Road, Ann Arbor, Michigan 48106-1346.

ISSN 0193-9416   ISBN 0-7879-1435-5

NEW DIRECTIONS FOR MENTAL HEALTH SERVICES is part of The Jossey-Bass Psychology Series and is published quarterly by Jossey-Bass Inc., 350 Sansome Street, San Francisco, California 94104-1342.

Subscriptions cost $65.00 for individuals and $110.00 for institutions, agencies, and libraries.

EDITORIAL CORRESPONDENCE should be sent to the Editor-in-Chief, H. Richard Lamb, University of Southern California, Department of Psychiatry, Graduate Hall, 1937 Hospital Place, Los Angeles, California 90033–1071.

Cover photograph by Wernher Krutein/PHOTOVAULT ©1990.

Jossey-Bass Web address: www.josseybass.com

Printed in the United States of America on acid-free recycled paper containing 100 percent recovered waste paper, of which at least 20 percent is postconsumer waste.

CONTENTS

EDITOR'S NOTES

In April 1997, the American Psychiatric Association appointed Paul Jay Fink (chair), Carl C. Bell (vice chair), Arthur Z. Berg, Sandra L. Bloom, Bradley R. Johnson, Sandra J. Kaplan, J. David Kinzie, Richard P. Kluft, John R. Lion, and Joe Tupin to the Council of National Affairs, Task Force on Psychiatric Aspects of Violence, which was staffed by Linda Roll. During our first few meetings it became apparent that the members of the task force had a veritable mental storehouse of knowledge regarding psychiatric viewpoints on violence and that I was in for a great education. Our charge was apparently an awesome one as we could liken psychiatric perspectives on violence to a complex lattice with many different facets that were interdependent and yet could stand alone. After we produced a rough draft to give to the American Psychiatric Association, we decided, as we had more useful material than we needed for that purpose, that we would produce this volume for *New Directions for Mental Health Services*. (The contents do not necessarily represent the position of the American Psychiatric Association; they represent the thoughts of the authors.)

In Chapter One, Tupin illustrates how biology influences the biopsychosocial multideterminate equation that produces some forms of violence. His brief review highlights what we currently know.

Chapter Two was developed from two separate efforts by Berg on one hand and Bell and Tupin on the other. Because of the synergy between the two efforts, we combined them to create the best of both worlds. It was the consensus of the group that we should support clinicians should they find the need to defend themselves against a patient attack. Although having to defend oneself physically against a patient attack is unsettling from a moral and legal perspective, the group decided to adopt Kluft's adage, "It is better to be judged by twelve than carried by six." Although related to clinician safety, assessing the risk for violence has a broader scope, and Johnson's chapter clarifies the various roles psychiatrists have regarding the prediction of violence.

The chapter by Kaplan covers all aspects of family violence. This is an important consideration as a vast amount of violence occurs in the interpersonal relationship. This chapter provides examples of family violence intervention programs, organizational policy statements and clinical guidelines, and victim advocacy and referral resources.

The group also decided to address both the victim and perpetrator aspects of sexual violence as mental health professionals are often confronted with treating both groups. Also, the truth is that victims may be at greater risk for becoming perpetrators. Accordingly, Bloom addresses the victim aspects of sexual violence and provides various Web sites and other resources to acknowledge this concern. Johnson covers perpetrator issues involved with sexual violence and covers assessment, treatment, and forensic issues; he also provides resources and recommendations for dealing with the sexually violent perpetrator.

Finally, the chapter on treating victims of violence is a long one, but it is filled with relevant, critical information. The high incidence of victimization in our society and the need to address this source of trauma makes this information essential.

Carl C. Bell
Editor

CARL C. BELL is professor of psychiatry and public health at the University of Illinois at Chicago and chief executive officer and president of the Community Mental Health Council and Foundation in Chicago.

1

As this decade of the brain unlocks the secrets of the mind, mental health professionals will gain a greater understanding of how biology shapes the biopsychosocial factors that generate some forms of violence.

The Biology of Violence

Joe Tupin

As the field of neuropsychiatry becomes more sophisticated, the mechanisms for some causes of violent behaviors will become known. Further, as the field develops, psychiatric treatment of some violent behaviors will become more specific. However, without developing the infrastructure to provide these more sophisticated services, communities with the greatest need will be the last to receive appropriate health care that can prevent some biological causes of violence. This section will discuss what psychiatry currently knows about biology and violence.

Congenital Factors

Genetic, prenatal, and perinatal factors are congenital biological variables that may increase an individual's risk for being violent.

Genetic. There are three lines of inquiry and evidence for the influence of genetics on violent behavior:

- Twin, family, and adoptive studies support the existence of a genetic contribution to aggression and violence in children and adults.
- Family and adoptive studies underscore that there is an environmental-genetic interaction.
- Molecular genetics has yet to identify a single or linear relationship, but it suggests further research is indicated to evaluate the contribution of specific genes to measurable elements of aggression and violence (Cadoret, Leve, and Devor, 1997).

Such research will need to be guided by hypotheses such as how genetic factors may underlie alterations in neurotransmitters and whether low central nervous system serotonin is related to violence symptoms. This research must also involve systematic work to examine synthesis, degradation, and receptors. Genetic exploration is necessary as it will reveal the importance of family and developmental history in cross-generational and childhood behaviors. Furthermore, although genetic research has not yet identified specifics to yield gene interventions, the data suggest the possibility of early recognition of high-risk individuals suitable for environmental interventions that may modify genetic propensities. The data may also portend the need to use pharmacological interventions for modifying genetic actions to reduce symptoms.

Prenatal and Perinatal. Prenatal events and birth complications alone do not clearly predict criminal or violent behaviors (Volavka, 1995). However, exposure of the fetus to alcohol has been linked to bullying and impulsiveness (Streissguth and others, 1991), and exposure to other central nervous system active agents such as cocaine may have similar effects. However, we need long-term, prospective studies to be sure. Prenatal and perinatal events likely interact with other elements, such as social class, parenting, or hyperactivity, resulting in increased childhood and adult aggressive and violent behaviors. Other than identifying fetal alcohol syndrome (FAS), there is not much independent information of diagnostic use. Early recognition of individuals with FAS might allow parenting interventions or medication use in affected individuals. However, prevention seems more appropriate and effective.

Neurochemistry Factors

Serotonin, norepinephrine, dopamine, GABA (gamma amino buteric acid), acetylcholine, and monoamine oxidase are considered related to aggressive or violent behavior in humans and animals (Eichelman and Hartwig, 1995; Volavka, 1995). A relative reduction of serotonin or an excess of norepinephrine, influenced by genetics, rearing, environment, and brain injury is linked to increased aggressiveness and violence. Collectively these studies remain exploratory: much of the work was done in animals, with different assessment techniques for these biochemical systems. Furthermore, because no objective description of violent behaviors has been developed, clinical correlation and cross-study consistency is impaired. Clinical descriptions of subjects studied for neurochemical abnormalities describe impulsivity, excess anger, and limited control; however, no systematic descriptive studies exist with biochemical correlates. Thus, to date, no clinically useful laboratory tests exist. Clinical necessity and research observations have produced useful experience with medications that interact with these biochemical systems, and some clinical trials have had beneficial effects on violent patients (see Chapter Two). Medication selection, which is limited and based on theories and empirical observations, has lead to the use of drugs thought to enhance serotonin effects, such as SSRIs (selective serotonin reuptake inhibitors), lithium, buspirone, and trazadone. Another approach is to use drugs to reduce adrenergic activity, usually with a beta-blocker such as propranolol, nadolol, or pindolol. The beta-blockers have been found particularly useful in patients with organic brain syndromes (Yudofsky, Williams, and Gorman, 1981). Clonidine, an alpha-adrenergic agonist, has been used successfully in children and adolescents with aggression linked to ADHD (attention deficit hyperactivity disorder), conduct disorders, and autism (Jaselskis, Cook, Fletcher, and Leventhal, 1992).

Neuroendocrine Factors

Although controversial, studies in this area have focused on sex hormones and to a limited degree insulin and blood sugar. Inconsistencies exist in human and animal studies, but research suggests that testosterone (the most widely studied) plays a role in violence and aggression. In humans, higher levels are found in violent criminals. Also, more aggressiveness is observed with relatively higher levels of testosterone, not necessarily abnormal levels. Although this hypothesis is in need of further research, the hypoglycemia studies suggest lower blood sugar is linked to irritability, impulsiveness, and violence. Also, premenstrual dysphoric disorder has been linked to irritability, anger, and increased interpersonal conflict. To date, no practical clinical information has developed from these studies other than to remind the clinician that relative increases in testosterone are linked to violence, particularly sexual aggression by males. Despite legal, ethical, and medical problems, methods of reducing testosterone levels have included drugs and surgery (rarely used). Although controversial, medroxyprogesterone acetate has been used at major specialized centers in various sexual offenders and may reduce sexual drive and dangerous behaviors. There are case reports of using buspirone for premenstrual syndrome (PMS).

Neuropathology Factors

Brain dysfunction has long been thought to have a role in irritable, impulsive, and violent behavior (Bell, 1986, 1987; Bell and Kelly, 1987; Volavka, 1995). Study methods have included neuroimaging, neuropsychology, clinical neurology, and electrophysiological studies. It has been learned that focal and diffuse abnormalities play a role in violent behavior. Localized lesions are more likely to be in the temporal lobes or the frontal lobes, but more often the dysfunction is determined to be diffuse or multisite. Etiology is variable and includes trauma, infection, heavy metals such as lead, tumors, and degenerative neurological disease such as Huntington's.

Electrophysiological disorders (especially temporal seizures) represent another group of dysfunctions thought to be related to violence. Although some controversy exists, it is unlikely that directed or purposeful violence is a direct manifestation of a seizure or the post-ictal period. During these times any aggressive behavior represents confusion or resistance to attempts to restrain the person. Inter-ictal behavior has also been studied with the conclusion that there may be some increase in aggression and violence during that time. Such an increase appears not to be related to the type of epilepsy. However, further study is needed to confirm these points of increased prevalence and relationship to the type of seizure.

An evaluation of violent individuals should include a careful history to evaluate neurological function, disease, and injury. Neuropsychological and neurological clinical evaluations are important using imaging and electroencephalographic (EEG) sleep studies as indicated. Violence linked to DSM-IV Axis I and II diagnoses may coexist with brain dysfunctions (Krakowski and Czobor, 1994). Accordingly, if standard treatment of Axis I or II does not reduce violence-linked behavior, a brain dysfunction should be considered. Surgery is rarely indicated but is obviously required for tumors or other structural lesions. Psychosurgery is controversial and rarely indicated. Surgery for seizure control has not been sufficiently evaluated for any possible effect on aggression. Medication use is nonspecific, but the literature reports it is effective in brain dysfunction patients who are violent. Anticonvulsants (carbamazepine and divalproex), lithium, beta-blockers (propranolol and others), serotonin enhancers (buspirone, trazadone, SSRIs), and clozapine have been used in this population. Unfortunately, few controlled, double-blind, and placebo studies exist. Typical, older antipsychotics are probably indicated only for short-term use for immediate control of aggressive behavior unless a psychosis exists. Recent reviews have suggested that the older antipsychotics have no special antiaggressive effect, only sedation. Divalproex sodium has been the most widely used anticonvulsant, and propranolol is the most commonly used beta-blocker. Short-term control in emergencies is often well managed with injectable benzodiazepines.

Toxicology and Substance Abuse

Drugs, both street and prescribed, may promote aggressiveness and violence. The undesired behavior may result either from the direct action of the drug or from withdrawal in the chronic user. Stimulants (amphetamines, cocaine), hallucinogens, and alcohol promote violence. Paradoxically, stimulants have been studied in a few subjects, presumably with ADHD, and their aggressiveness has decreased (Klein and others, 1997). Some newer street drugs have been linked to violence. Prescribed drugs such as anticholinergics and meperidine may cause violence, usually by toxic effects producing confusion. Some investigators have suggested that akathisia from antipsychotics may produce aggression. Withdrawal from sedative drugs often produces confusion and agitation with dangerous behavior.

References

Bell, C. C. "Coma and the Etiology of Violence, Part 1." *Journal of the National Medical Association,* 1986, *78*(12), 1167–1176.

Bell, C. C. "Coma and the Etiology of Violence, Part 2." *Journal of the National Medical Association,* 1987, *79*(1), 79–85.

Bell, C. C., and Kelly, R. "Head Injury with Subsequent Intermittent, Non-Schizophrenic, Psychotic Symptoms and Violence." *Journal of the National Medical Association,* 1987, *79*(11), 1139–1144.

Cadoret, R. J., Leve, L. D., and Devor, E. "Genetics of Aggressive and Violent Behavior." *Psychiatric Clinics of North America,* 1997, *20*(2), 301–322.

Eichelman, B. S., and Hartwig, A. C. (eds.). *Patient Violence and the Clinician.* Washington, D.C.: American Psychiatric Press, 1995.

Jaselskis, C. A., Cook, E. H., Fletcher, K. E., and Leventhal, B. L. "Clonidine Treatment of Hyperactive and Impulsive Children with Autistic Disorder." *Journal of Clinical Psychopharmacology,* 1992, *12*(5), 322–327.

Klein, R. G., and others. "Clinical Efficacy of Methylphenidate in Conduct Disorder with and Without Attention Deficit Hyperactivity Disorder." *Archives of General Psychiatry,* 1997, *54,* 1073–1080.

Krakowski, M. I., and Czobor, P. "Clinical Symptoms, Neurological Impairment, and Prediction of Violence in Psychiatric Inpatients." *Hospital and Community Psychiatry,* 1994, *45,* 700–705.

Streissguth, A. P., and others. "Fetal Alcohol Syndrome in Adolescents and Adults." *Journal of the American Medical Association,* 1991, *265*(15), 1961–1967.

Volavka, J. *Neurobiology of Violence.* Washington, D.C.: *American Psychiatric Press,* 1995.

Yudofsky, S., Williams, D., and Gorman, J. "Propranolol in the Treatment of Rage and Violent Behavior in Patients with Chronic Brain Syndromes." *American Journal of Psychiatry,* 1981, *138*(2), 218–220.

Joe Tupin is professor emeritus of psychiatry at the University of California, Davis, and medical director emeritus at the University of California, Davis, Medical Center.

2

Many clinicians deny the possibility of violence occurring in their practices, and this denial has its roots in fear of violence or overconfidence in safety. To appropriately address the issue of violence, clinicians must engage in proactive behaviors and attitudes that will ensure their safety.

Clinician Safety: Assessing and Managing the Violent Patient

Arthur Z. Berg, Carl C. Bell, Joe Tupin

Eventually, all relationships must address the issue of aggression, and the relationship between mental health professional and patient is no different. Because clinicians frequently choose their profession to relieve suffering, and conceive of the role as nurturing and supportive, a patient's aggression is frequently a surprise. Many patients who go to clinicians need nurturing and supportive therapeutic relationships. Unfortunately, many others need help in controlling behavior that may be excessively aggressive. This being the case, clinicians must have a thorough understanding about violence and develop appropriate attitudes regarding various forms of violence (Baker and Bell, 1999). Although a clinician's mission may be to save lives, lessen suffering, and do no harm, to fulfill this mission the healer must be safe from harm.

Denial

A crucial aspect of psychiatric training is learning how to ensure safety. Thus clinicians need skills in assessing and managing the violent patient. We often overlook this aspect of psychiatric training or give it minimal attention. Denial is the primary reason for the lack of institutional concern that results from ignoring the need for safety training. Denial also plays a role in clinicians' missing danger signs or overestimating their ability to cope with potential violence. This denial may have its roots in experiences with violence or may come from a lack of exposure to violence (Berg, 1997).

The purpose of this chapter is to highlight some paradigmatic principles that should act as guidelines for clinicians who are being attacked or confronted by imminently violent and potentially violent patients. The chapter covers issues of personal safety and the management of three levels of violence.

Scope of the Problem

Mental health care providers are at great risk of being attacked by patients.

Prevalence of Violent Incidents in the Mentally Ill. Using National Institute of Mental Health Epidemiologic Catchment Area study data, Swanson, Holzer, Ganju, and Jono (1990) reviewed the incidence of violent behavior during the previous year. They found that the prevalence of violence was five times greater among people who met an Axis I diagnosis than it was among interviewees who were not diagnosable. Furthermore, violence prevalence among persons with a diagnosis of alcoholism or drug abuse was twelve and sixteen times greater, respectively, than it was in subjects who were not diagnosable (Swanson, Holzer, Ganju, and Jono, 1990). It has also been found that co-occurring substance abuse disorder markedly increases the likelihood of violence in patients with a major mental illness, with 31 percent committing at least one act of violence during a one-year follow-up (Steadman and others, 1998). Accordingly, because psychiatry treats patients who have a greater likelihood of perpetrating violence, providing mental health care is a high-risk profession.

Frequency of Assaults on Clinicians. Caretakers and nursing staff are frequent targets of assault. However, physicians are not far behind. The rate of victimization of mental health professionals in the workplace from 1992 to 1996 was 79.5 per 1,000. The rate of victimization of physicians in the workplace from 1992 to 1996 was 15.7 per 1,000 (Bureau of Justice Statistics, 1998). Workplace homicide rates for psychiatrists and mental health professionals are exceeded only by those for taxi drivers, convenience store clerks, and police officers (U.S. Department of Health and Human Services, 1993). Examining the available literature on violence in the health care setting, Tardiff (1987) notes that approximately 40 percent of psychiatrists have been assaulted at some time during their careers, and 48 percent of psychiatric residents are assaulted during residency. In one documented study of eighteen physicians murdered by patients, seven were psychiatrists (Ladds and Lion, 1996). Furthermore, 80 percent of all nurses are assaulted at least once during their careers, resulting in a higher rate of occupational violence than found in any other workplace (Occupational Safety and Health Administration, 1996). Psychiatric nursing staff members experience an even higher rate of assault with more serious injury. Injuries range from bruises to bone fractures and head trauma, and they include rape and homicide. The psychological and economic cost of this workplace violence in mental health settings is staggering. Administrative costs compound the monetary costs of death, injury, and psychological damage. These include lost workdays, staff recruitment and turnover, security, police, investigations, litigation, and worker's compensation.

Many of these assaults are preventable: education and safety training significantly reduce the risk. We must provide safety training quarterly, as we do with cardiopulmonary resuscitation (CPR) and fire drills. Such training must emphasize awareness of risk, principles of managing aggressive behavior, and instruction in self-defense. Like CPR, self-defense instruction must be hands-on and given by qualified instructors.

Personal Safety and Attitudes About Aggression and Violence

When confronted with an aggressive, potentially violent patient, personal safety should always be a prime concern. Unfortunately, because of clinician experiences and attitudes, this concern may not be manifest. Clinicians must have appropriate attitudes regarding violence and follow some basic principles to maintain personal safety. Consequently, mental health leadership must place the issue of personal safety in the consciousness of clinicians and emphasize the staff's right to personal safety. Administrators should tell practitioners that they have a right to defend themselves when threatened with bodily harm. Such an assertion removes some potential immobilizing ambivalence or confusion about how to proceed if attacked.

Clinician Experiences with Violence

Once practitioners have openly embraced the value of personal safety, proper supervision and training can correct the hindrances that make them effective and efficient in managing potentially violent patients. Additionally, supervision can build upon assets in staff to make them more competent and capable of handling violent individuals. Clinician experiences and attitudes may also be a strength in appropriately assessing and treating the violent individual. Therefore, practitioners should explore and address those experiences with trauma and violence that might influence their judgment. Clinician exposure to trauma and violence may be quite high. For example, one study of social service providers found that 3 percent reported being physically assaulted and 7 percent reported being robbed in the past year. Furthermore, 9 percent reported being raped, 11 percent reported being shot at—with 3 percent of these being hit—and 3 percent reported having been stabbed. Regarding witnessing violence, 25 percent reported seeing someone get shot, 25 percent reported seeing someone stabbed, and 11 percent reported seeing someone killed. Finally, 55 percent reported knowing someone who was murdered, and 48 percent reported knowing someone who was raped. Only 3 percent reported ever being counseled (Bell, Mock, and Slutkin, forthcoming).

Hierarchy of Aggression

Exploring clinicians' experiences with violence helps practitioners understand that although violence is aggressive not all aggression is violent and thus aggression requires different approaches. Table 1.1 defines the hierarchy of aggression further. Having some understanding of this hierarchy helps structure the clinician's response to the various levels of aggression appropriately. Clinicians should understand that hostility may result from the need to obtain a goal (bullying the doctor to get drugs) or the need to hurt or destroy anything that frustrates a goal-directed activity such as self-assertion, exploration, or dominance. Furthermore, hostility may come from the need to protect oneself from injury (caused by a threat or actual trauma), and once the perceived injury is addressed, the hostility abates.

Table 1.1. Hierarchy of Aggression

1. Lowest level of aggression	1. Alertness, initiative, curiosity, motivation, attentiveness, and exploratory behavior.
2. Self-assertion	2. The attempt to establish, maintain, and expand one's boundaries and integrity while not intruding into others' territory.
3. Dominance	3. The capacity to exert an influence on the behavior of other people or groups in an intended direction (also known as power). Dominance tends to be grounded in coercion—that is, it creates expectation of great rewards or great punishments for certain kinds of behavior.
a. Authority	a. Dominance that is legitimized by legal, professional, or social mores
i. Legitimate	i. Conferred by virtue of a law or formal designation
ii. Charismatic	ii. Bestowed by virtue of having "winning ways with people"
iii. Traditional	iii. Granted out of respect for elders
iv. Mission driven	iv. Accorded by group consensus regarding the purpose of a body
4. Hostility	4. Behavior or attitudes intending to hurt or destroy an object or the self.
a. Violence	a. The use of force to physically injure
5. Hatred	5. The injury or destruction of an object, self, or situation is the end rather than the means to an end.

Source: Parts of this table are adapted from Marcovitz, 1973.

Clinician Attitudes

In addition to understanding a hierarchy of aggression, clinicians should explore their attitudes and affects, as such attitudes and affects effect patients' responses to mental health professionals. Examples of such attitudes and affects include

Fearful, submissive, and excessively permissive
Brave and overconfident
Excessively aggressive, controlling, and strict
Counterphobic
Detached or avoidant
Concerned
Actively friendly (gregarious)
Passively friendly (helpful but not intrusive)
Matter-of-fact

Overview of Best Practices

Once clinicians have consciously made an investment in their personal safety, explored their attitudes about violence, and explored their affects toward violent situations, they can pursue best practices to maximize their safety.

Assessment. Assessing the cause of violence is important information that is useful for managing violent patients. Various studies have shown that individuals with certain mental disorders are more likely to be violent than others. These are patients who are

Withdrawing from drugs or alcohol
Suffering from chronic organic brain damage resulting in impulsivity
Suffering from acute organic brain syndromes resulting in deliriousness
Acutely ill (paranoid patients who feel threatened; manic patients who are agitated; depressed patients who are explosive)
Suffering from borderline, antisocial, or paranoid personality disorders (Tardiff, 1984; Reid and Balis, 1987)

Consequently, time permitting, management of the violent patient usually begins with special attention to diagnosis.

Timing. Assessment of the cause of violence is facilitated or hindered by the amount of time available. Clearly, while one is being choked is not the time to gather data about why one is being choked. Being choked calls for a physical response. Thus the immediacy of the situation is more important than assessing the cause of violence and is the main principle for managing violence. Therefore we can categorize violence as potential, urgent or imminent, and emergent (Tupin, 1983).

Summary of Best Practices

Managing violence based on the amount of time available to respond is the best practice. Consultation is a critical tool in managing potentially violent patients. Identifying patients with more potential for violence than other patients is also important. Clinician safety also involves awareness of potentially violent situations and settings. Furthermore, clinicians must know how to manage potentially violent patients by maintaining an environmental protective shield and using medication before violence erupts. Clinicians must also be aware of warning signs of escalation leading to imminent violence and must know how to manage imminent violence by de-escalating the imminently violent patient. Additionally, if they are unable to de-escalate imminent violence, clinicians need to know how to manage emergent violent behavior using safety and rescue equipment, self-defense, and a coordinated response to violence or assault. Education and training in violence management are critical tools in maintaining clinician safety and should not be overlooked. Lastly, reporting violence and assaults and collecting accurate statistics is vitally important if we are to understand the patterns of violence comprehensively.

Potential Violence

Although certain categories of patients are at greater risk for perpetrating violence, as discussed earlier (Swanson, Holzer, Ganju, and Jono, 1990), patients with a history of violence should be considered at an even greater risk for being violent again. Thus potentially violent patients are individuals who have a history of violence but who are not currently threatening to become violent. In this situation there is time to plan how to respond to the patient's violence should it manifest itself.

Consultation. Consultation during treatment of violence-prone individuals is crucial and may be life saving. Fear, countertransference difficulties, denial, and unrecognized provocative behavior by a therapist or staff member may interfere with good clinical judgment. The therapist and staff may distance themselves from the patient, ignore threats, or overreact and overcontrol. The consultation may be formal or part of ongoing supervision. It may be informal discussion with colleagues, supervisors, or other staff members. It is important that feelings about a patient be discussed. Feelings about a violence-prone patient may include fear, anger, or inappropriate neutrality. In a hospital setting, there should be regularly scheduled staff meetings to discuss violent or potentially violent patients. Staff members should be encouraged to express their feelings. Having such meetings before the admission of violence-prone patients is sometimes useful. This may prevent negative expectations and subsequent distancing by staff. It may prevent overcontrol, which leads to unnecessary use of restraint and seclusion, prolonged length of stay, or excessive use of medication.

Identifying Potentially Violent Patients. Identifying potentially violent individuals is done by obtaining a thorough history of violence (Tardiff, 1984; Reid and Balis, 1987). Such patients can also be identified by conducting background checks through police records for occurrences of assault (see Chapter Three). Such investigations reveal that some patients are repetitively violent whereas others have isolated incidents of violence. An important aspect of gathering a history of violence is determining the patient's violence triggers. Research on violent patients reveals that patients with a history of a psychosis who have isolated incidents of violence have their episode of violence while in the throes of an acute decompensation (Mulvey, 1994). Alternatively, patients with a history of a psychosis who have persistent episodes of violence are patients who also have neurological impairment (Krakowski and Czobor, 1994). Fortunately, the standard of violence prediction is not as stringent in real life as it is in the forensic setting (see Chapter Three). As a result, the clinician can maintain a high index of caution when treating patients with certain diagnoses or problems. A history of violence remains the most reliable predictor of future violence (Brizer, 1989). However, new research based on actuarial data may soon provide tools for predicting potentially violent patients (Hare, 1991; Harris and Rice, 1997).

Awareness of Potentially Violent Situations and Settings. General conditions that increase the risk of harmful assault are

Alcohol or drug abuse
Insufficient staff
Untrained security personnel or lack of emergency devices
Unsafe architectural layouts, an inability to observe, lack of escape routes
Furniture or objects that could be used as weapons
Disquieting or otherwise unpleasant living arrangements for patients or staff

Specific situations that signal an increased risk of violent assault are

Limit setting with explosive patients: placing or removing patients from restraints, for example
Interviewing for fitness to return to duty or discharge from employment
Interviewing spouses or children in domestic abuse cases
Being informed that an unfamiliar person has been seen loitering or observing or otherwise appearing at one's home or office
Having a patient appear at inappropriate times or places
Receiving unusual phone calls or mail
Feeling any apprehension or fear that is otherwise unexplainable (De Becker, 1997)

Furthermore, the possibility of having to manage a violent patient is more likely in certain locations than in others. These settings are emergency rooms, crisis clinics, admission units, intensive care units, and detoxification units.

In high-risk situations or settings, mental health professionals should cultivate an increased level of conscious awareness of potentially dangerous situations. Recognizing risk factors for potential violence is a critical skill that aids prevention and safety; thus a sustained level of alertness is required. This level of alertness, referred to by the police and military as condition yellow, is different from having a high index of suspicion or being in red alert. It requires a constant awareness of immediate surroundings—in front, alongside, in back. This is the same level of awareness necessary to drive a car defensively. It is a physiologically healthy, nonparanoid state that enhances the clinical skill of observation. It is neither a totally relaxed nor a hyperalert state, but it is a state of attentiveness to warning signs.

Violent and even lethal confrontations may also occur with dangerous persons not known to the clinician. Mental health professionals may become targets of

Persons involved in civil or criminal litigation with a patient
Physical and sexual abusers of patients in treatment
Spouses or partners of patients in child custody disputes
Persons with an erotomanic fixation on a patient
Another clinician's patient who includes others in a delusional system

These persons may perceive the treating or testifying professional as responsible for an undesirable outcome. This can be dangerous. The usual first lines of defense may be insufficient. Hospitalization may not be available. The police and the judicial system may not be able to intervene.

In these instances there may be warnings such as spoken or written threats or stalking. The following actions should be taken: (1) The clinician should obtain special threat management consultation. Unless police departments or psychiatrists have special expertise in this area, they should not be relied upon to assess threats. Experts in this area should be consulted. A coordinated plan with increased security measures may be required. (2) There should be evaluation of the use of restraining orders. However, restraining orders may not suffice or may be contraindicated. Restraining orders may precipitate a violent reaction, as they sometimes do in domestic abuse situations.

There should be no response to any communication, written or spoken, until expert consultation, risk evaluation, and a coordinated security plan have been undertaken. The plan will include appropriate countermeasures. Exact copies and details of all communications should be retained. These are extremely useful to experts in evaluating risk and devising a security plan.

Environmental Protective Shield: Physical and Emotional. Given that some settings are more dangerous than others, creating an environment that prevents violence is an effective approach (Lion, Dubin, and Futrell, 1996; Colling, 1996). By reestablishing a protective shield, previously traumatized individuals will feel safe (Pynoos and Nader, 1988) and less reactive to perceived injury. The setting and previous levels of violence, based on an analysis of incident reports, determine the degree of protective shield needed.

Clinical interviews occur in private offices in homes or commercial buildings where clinicians are solely responsible for their own safety. In these settings the following precautions should be observed. Patients with a history of violence or paranoia or who are borderline with little impulse control should not be seen here. A more secure setting such as a hospital emergency ward or an office with available psychiatric and security staff is indicated. Although private office comfort and attractiveness are important considerations, complacency and denial should not preclude safety. In addition, a call button that sounds in a reception area or at a neighbor's can be discreetly placed even in the plushest of offices. A small, well-designed one-way mirror may be disguised in a wall or door to check on potentially violent visitors. A spring-locked door that can be closed quickly and securely is useful in handling an unexpected surprise when the waiting room door is opened.

The physical structure of the clinic milieu can also be a great deterrent against violence. Having windows in doors of examining rooms allows privacy while also lending a sense of the possibility of being monitored for unacceptable behavior. Security cameras also provide a sense that behavior is being monitored. Posting rules in the clinic that make it clear that violence will not be tolerated and has consequences is another useful strategy. Preventing areas of relative seclusion from being used for examination purposes can also decrease the use of unmonitored areas that sometimes gives tacit approval for unacceptable behavior. Finally, removing potential weapons, such as scissors, from the clinic office is also a preventive strategy for managing potentially violent patients.

Although offices in emergency rooms and on psychiatric wards should be comfortable and attractive, additional security measures are required. For example, furniture should not block egress and should be heavy or soft so that it cannot be used as a weapon. Similarly, desk and decorative objects such as letter openers and sculptures can be used as weapons. They should not be accessible. Additionally, when potentially violent patients are being treated, security personnel may be positioned outside the office door or clinicians may leave the door open. There should be no spring-loaded locks on these doors. Imminently violent patients may require the presence of other staff or security personnel in the office. In extreme cases, patients may have to be interviewed while in restraints. In addition, a security presence should be visible when patients enter a clinic setting.

Nursing stations and break areas, as well as offices, must be equipped with panic buttons. Personal emergency call devices should be provided to staff members. Restraining equipment, including ambulatory restraints and properly designed seclusion rooms, must be available. Visible restraint cots in psychiatric emergency settings may also send a message that out-of-control behavior is not tolerated. A sense of a protective shield can be established by having patients walk through a portal metal detector or searched before they are examined in an emergency room setting (Bell and Palmer, 1981). Emergency medications should be readily available (see Chapter One).

The physical layouts of psychiatric units require specialized planning. Safety features include traffic patterns, patient visibility, and placement of communications and alarms. Access, window construction, and living-area fixtures require special attention. Plate glass can be broken and used as a deadly weapon. Shower heads can be used for suicide attempts or removed and used as weapons. Forensic units and emergency wards have special security needs. They may require magnetometer screening devices to prevent introduction of weapons. They may require increased security personnel, physical barriers, and sophisticated surveillance devices.

The emotional and attitudinal work environment can also prevent violence. Milieus characterized by good teamwork and interdependence present unified fronts against the likelihood of violence. Furthermore, management styles that encourage the establishment and maintenance of good relationships will encourage staff to continue these practices toward patients, and such practices encourage a "connectedness" that has been shown to discourage various violent behaviors (Resnick and others, 1997). Good relationships allow for sensitivity to patients' psychological injuries, which are frequently at the root of violent behavior. Such relationships also help staff in talking a patient down from an agitated, escalating state. Furthermore, such relationships assist in maintaining respect for patient boundaries, the transgression of which may trigger a violent attack.

Uses of Medication in Potentially Violent Patients. Using medication to control target symptoms that promote violence is a useful strategy to prevent violence (Hughes, 1999). For long-term care, medication is often effective in reducing or controlling violence (Tardiff, 1999). Potentially violent patients require careful study to determine if any treatable pathological processes are underlying the violence, and DSM-IV diagnosis (Axes I, II, and III) may be relevant. In particular, note those conditions that have violence as an essential feature, such as intermittent explosive disorder, sexual sadism, and those conditions that have violence as an associated feature, including organic mental disorder and posttraumatic stress disorder (Menninger, 1993). If violence is a direct product of a DSM-IV disorder, medication should be selected to treat that disorder—antipsychotics for schizophrenia-determined violence, for example. However, violence in schizophrenics may also result from coexisting brain injury or substance abuse. In these cases another medication must be added to the antipsychotic.

Antipsychotics do not have a specific antiviolence effect, and akathisia associated with high-potency medications has been linked to violent behavior. Benzodiazepines have limited application to manage chronic violence. Although unstudied, they might be helpful in managing violence linked to anxiety. Other antianxiety agents have not been reported to be effective, but buspirone has been noted in case reports to be useful in patients with dementia, traumatic brain injury, and similar conditions. The initial effect may be to increase violence, and the benefit may take several weeks. As central nervous system serotonin availability is thought to be linked to reducing violence, antidepressant medications that increase serotonin are considered useful for the management of chronic violence (Bass and Beltis, 1991; Coccaro, Astill, Herbert, and Schut, 1990; Roy-Byrne and Fann, 1997). Older medications such as trazadone and amitriptyline have been found useful, and patients with brain injury may be good candidates. Antimanic agents such as lithium have been studied in different populations and found effective in conditions other than bipolar disorder, such as brain injury and mental retardation. Those who respond typically are explosive and easily provoked, respond with excessive violence, and may or may not be remorseful (Tupin, 1978). Anticonvulsants have been studied generally in open clinical protocols. Carbamazepine has been reported to be effective for patients with violence and seizures and other organic conditions. Valproic acid has also been used successfully. Antihypertensive medications (beta-blockers), particularly propranolol, have been studied and found useful in patients with organic brain syndromes, although clinical effects may take six to eight weeks (see Chapter One).

Imminent Violence

Situations are urgent when patients threaten imminent violence. These situations occur when an individual is escalating and about to commit violence but has not yet acted. In this situation there is some time to intervene but not a great deal of time. Such situations should be easy to identify.

Warning Signs of Imminent Violence. Mental health professionals should be aware of warning signs of imminent violence. Such signs consist of

Agitated behavior such as pacing
Threats that are explicit or implicit: spoken, written, or made via gestures
Body movements, especially of the extremities, such as the opening and closing of fists
Eye movement and appearance such as dilation or darting
Proximity, such as when a patient invades a clinician's personal space
Impulsiveness or the inability to comply with reasonable limit setting
A recent episode of violent or assaultive behavior
Fear in the clinician or any otherwise unexplained feeling of apprehension

Warning signs call for action: clinicians are more likely to be harmed when they ignore warning signs because of uncertainty, inexperience, or a false sense of bravado.

Spoken threats are the most frequent warning sign. The context in which a patient makes the threat is the most important factor in assessing the likelihood of aggressive or assaultive behavior. Spoken threats require immediate action when they take place in the following contexts:

Loud outbursts, name calling, and cursing that are increasing in intensity
Agitation, pacing, clenching fists
Drug or alcohol intoxication

These conditions indicate impending loss of control. Immediate de-escalation and other safety measures must be taken. The clinician may have to leave the area. If the verbal content is primarily vulgar and directed at everyone and everything, without an escalation or specific threat, aggressive behavior is still possible but less likely. Spoken threats expressed in a matter-of-fact, unemotional tone can also be dangerous. They require assessment and response, because, even though behavior is not escalating, these threats may portend future violence or assault. Threats made in the context of a psychosis are especially dangerous in the presence of

Agitation
Suicidal thought or behavior
Paranoid delusions, particularly those incorporating therapists or staff
A command voice or other control hallucinations

De-Escalation Using Clinical Skills. Observation of behavior that is escalating toward violence calls for an immediate verbal intervention designed to calm the patient down and de-escalate the situation from urgent or imminent to potential. Thus the ability to de-escalate and "calm down" an agitated or threatening person is basic for all clinicians (Walker, 1983). Usually, using interpersonal relationship skills to quickly establish a relationship or to build on an existing relationship is a useful strategy. Making it clear to the patient that the clinician is empathic toward the patient and wants to help the patient address the source of agitation or anger is necessary for a win-win outcome. Problem solving with the patient on how to address the source of agitation or anger will empower the patient and decrease the injury generating the anger. De-escalating has three components:

Verbal: what is said and how it is said are critical
Space: respecting the patient's sense of personal space
Body language: nonthreatening positions, gestures, and movements

With an emotionally escalating patient, the object of verbal intervention is to decrease the patient's underlying feelings of fear, inadequacy, and hopelessness. Volume, tone, and rate of speech should be lower than the patient's. (Although if it is too low, the patient may perceive it as a threat.) Assure the patient that he or she is understood. The patient should be listened to actively, with sufficient, nonintimidating eye contact. Statements should paraphrase the patient's statements to underscore that he or she is understood. All statements must be honest and precise. If not, they may encourage increased escalation. The goal is to encourage the patient to model the clinician's behavior and have a calmer interaction. Redirection of the conversation to less charged subjects may be occasionally helpful. Verbal limit setting, but not in an authoritative threatening manner, may be appropriate. Explain the rules of the milieu or the real consequences of the behavior. The fact that the behavior is frightening to you and others should be expressed. It may help decrease the patient's fear. Suggestions for increasing the patient's sense of safety include moving to a less threatening area; assuming seated, less threatening positions; and offering food or drink.

An escalating patient's personal space must be respected. When patients are agitated or threatened, their perceived zone of personal space increases, as does the fear of its being invaded. This personal space can be visualized as an oval zone extending four to six feet all around. Intrusion into that space will increase fear and thus the likelihood of assault. Remaining outside the oval zone of personal space also allows the clinician time to react to any assault. Approaching an escalating person should be made from the front or side as an approach from behind is extremely threatening. The clinician should never turn his or her back to the agitated or threatening patient.

As a patient's hospital room or living area may be regarded as personal space, request permission before entering. Escape routes, for the patient and the clinician, must not be blocked. If possible, the de-escalation should take place away from other patients or any atmosphere likely to overstimulate. Other staff should be present to assist, if necessary.

A show of force is sometimes necessary and may effectively preclude the need to escalate to physical restraint. The aggressive person will frequently capitulate in the presence of perceived overwhelming odds. A show of force may also increase the patient's sense of safety and control. If a show of force is employed, the patient must not be made to feel cornered or that his or her personal space is invaded.

The agitated, escalating patient is extremely sensitive to body language. The clinician's general demeanor, including posture and movements, is important. Nonaggressive stances and gestures are perceived as less threatening. They are also powerful tools for getting the patient to model the clinician's calmer attitude. One example of a nonthreatening position is to hold the hands at waist level with the palms up and open. The Thinker stance (one forearm crosses the chest, the opposite elbow rests on it with the index finger of that hand on the cheek or chin) is also nonthreatening. Any position that makes the clinician appear smaller, thus less threatening, is the object. Do not touch the patient or startle him or her with sudden movement, even to reassure. The clinician's body should be at a forty-five-degree angle to the disturbed patient. This keeps more of the clinician's body out of personal space and allows a larger reactionary gap in case of sudden assault. It also permits better balance and position if defensive or evasive movement is needed.

The ability to de-escalate requires practice in training situations. It requires practice to withstand an intense verbal barrage with a calm demeanor. It requires training to learn when a de-escalation should not be attempted. In some instances it may be good clinical judgment to leave the area.

De-Escalation Using Medication. Urgent situations will benefit from sedating medications for short-term control of violence. Short-term control of imminent violence by medication relies on the sedative effects of sedative benzodiazepines or high-potency neuroleptics (Tardiff, 1999). An agitated or imminently violent patient may accept oral medication instead of an injection. Haloperidol is a commonly used and effective drug. It is administered in five milligram doses intramuscularly (IM) or via a slow-push intravenous line (IV). The dose may be repeated every twenty to thirty minutes as needed. If the patient has not responded after two doses, benzodiazepine may be added. This combination is usually effective and may have fewer side effects than higher doses of either drug alone. Lorazepam is a preferred benzodiazepine because it may be given intramuscularly or by slow-push IV (Saltzman and others, 1991). It may be administered alone or in combination with haloperidol, as above. The dose is one or two milligrams every twenty to thirty minutes until the patient is calm. Deeper sedation is usually not required or desirable. The effectiveness of these medications is not an indication for their long-term use. Administration of either of these two types of medications should be limited to a few weeks unless a specific diagnosis is identified that justifies continuation. They should be discontinued once the crisis subsides. Long-term medication, if any, is dependent on the underlying psychiatric or medical diagnosis. Drugs used for long-term management of aggressive or violent behaviors are usually not effective in emergencies. Causing a paradoxical disinhibition syndrome is rare for benzodiazepines. If the patient has a known history of that reaction, a neuroleptic is used. If the patient is agitated or violent as a result of alcohol withdrawal or is known to have a seizure history, neuroleptics are avoided. They might lower seizure thresholds. Haloperidol, although safe, has not been approved by the Food and Drug Administration for IV use. Restricting that use to settings with monitoring capability, such as hospital units and emergency wards, is best. (See Chapter One.)

Emergent Violence

Emergent violence occurs when patients are being overtly violent. When the patient's violence is emerging there is no time to prevent violence. This is a time for escape. This is a time for calling for help. This is a time for restraining the patient, guided by a coordinated response. In more critical situations, self-defense may be appropriate. Emergent situations call for the non-specific sedating effects of either antipsychotics or benzodiazepines following the guidelines described above, except that parenteral administration will often be required.

With emergent violence there is no time to plan, and the intervention has to be physical in nature. If attacked by an assailant who does not have a weapon, a good strategy is to clinch, or bear hug, the individual the same way boxers do when they get into trouble in the ring. Just hold on as tight and close as possible and let patients tire themselves out (watch out for biting). This is also a good strategy even if the individual is using a striking weapon such as a club or a chair.

Once a physical attack has been spent, it is a good idea to restrain the patient or put the patient in restraints. Ideally, five people should help restrain a patient. However, in the event there are not enough people, and patient violence is dangerous, self-defense strategies and joint immobilization techniques may be necessary. The bigger the area in which the restraining occurs the better. Aikido training is probably the best martial art to study to become an expert in restraining patients (Westbrook and Ratti, 1974; Tohei, 1975).

Once violence has occurred and the crisis is over, the staff needs to do an autopsy to understand what happened, debrief to reduce tension of those involved, and plan how to respond more effectively, if possible. Critical incident debriefing is a standardized, easily learned technique that can be used to help staff recover from workplace violence. Incident reports need to be filled out and reviewed regularly to detect any weaknesses in the management of violent individuals.

Safety and Rescue Equipment.   Physical restraint devices, for restraining two or all four extremities, should be available in psychiatric and emergency department settings. Posey torso devices can accomplish restraint in a bed or a chair. Ambulatory restraints, such as protective aggression devices, can prevent arm strikes yet allow the patient to walk about (Maier, Van Rybroek, and Mays, 1994). The devices can be adjusted and tethered to control extent of movement.

Seclusion rooms are a safety device to protect staff from violent patients. They also provide the patient with a sense of safety and control. Seclusion areas must be scrupulously designed to avoid any danger. They must be constructed so patients cannot pull up floorboards, plaster sections, nails, or other dangerous materials. As violent patients may be suicidal, lighting and electrical outlets must not be accessible. There can be no structure or fixture on which a patient might hang himself or herself.

Having a written protocol for use of restraints and seclusion is essential. It is equally important that staff have adequate training in their use. The greatest number of staff injuries occurs during the placing and removing of physical restraints and during patient *take downs* with and without the use of a blanket or mattress. These events also account for the largest incidence of patient injuries.

Nonlethal sprays are effective safety and rescue devices. Hospital security staff use them. They can subdue otherwise unmanageable assaultive behavior, deter without needing to be discharged, and effect rescue in emergency hostage situations. Oleoresin capsicum (OC), or pepper spray, is effective. Mace, CN (omega-chloracephenone), and tear gas are not effective as they have delayed reaction time and are potentially dangerous. Their use is for crowd control. Use of nonlethal sprays by psychiatric staff, as opposed to security personnel, is controversial. However, emergencies cannot always wait for security personnel. Clinicians have the option of carrying an OC device in their private practices and off duty. Certification in its use requires only a two-hour course.

Self-Defense. We cannot always anticipate or prevent violent, harmful, or lethal assault. In these rare events, we may require spontaneous reaction to survive. Complacency and denial usually result in fatality. As with anticipated assaults, the responsible clinician will have a prearranged plan. That plan could include brief professional instruction or lectures in self-defense. We cannot effectively learn reflexive defensive reactions from a book. Courses and lectures are useful for clinicians of both sexes and of all ages and physical conditions.

In an anticipated attack, a few deep, slow breaths decrease anxiety and provide a moment to prepare. In unanticipated attack, holding one's breath, a usual reaction to acute stress or panic, promotes "freezing" and diminishes clarity, strength, and endurance. We can visualize defensive reaction scenarios for most settings in professional and private life. This also helps reduce the freeze reaction should the unthinkable happen. A most important fundamental is that effective self-defense requires a predetermined decision that an all-out effort will be made until the attacker is incapacitated, help arrives, or there is a completely safe method of escape. The idea of harming someone is foreign to most mental health workers. Nonviolent methods that do not cause harm are appropriate for management of aggressive patients. But when faced with serious bodily injury or death, those methods may not apply. The clinician must be prepared to do whatever violence is necessary to save himself or herself and others. In these situations, "First, do no harm" has no place.

Coordinated Response to Violence and Assault. Psychiatric facilities should have a written protocol that addresses

Responding to overt violence, de-escalating impending violence, and flagging potentially violent patients (the latter is especially useful with computerized records)

Identifying warning signs of impending violence

Responding to specific indications with coordinated methods, usually through a designated staff team that is skilled and practiced in managing overtly violent patients (de-escalation, escort techniques, use of restrain-

ing devices, patient control with use of blankets or a mattress, and proper
show of force procedures)
Education and training in understanding violence, violence safety, and self-
defense
Policies and practices for maintaining safe environments
A quality assurance system designed to monitor violence and take correc-
tive action

Emphasis should be on

Decreasing disquieting or otherwise unpleasant environments for patients
and staff
Establishing a solid rapport with the patient
Using medication to prevent violence
Respecting the patient's sense of space and value
Developing a plan with the family member for safety and intervention
Warning individuals about dangerous patients
Ensuring that interview rooms are safe
Ensuring a sense of security in the clinical setting
Developing a plan to manage patients with weapons

Agency security personnel must be well trained in the management of
aggressive behavior (Maier, 1996). Security personnel and the staff response
team should function as a coordinated unit with everybody—physicians
included—practicing drills (Colling, 1995).

As part of the coordinated response, the administration must promote
training, collect statistical data, and provide support to involved staff or visitors. The administration may need to deal with potential litigation or treatment plans that call for prosecution of a patient who has threatened or
assaulted. The administration is also responsible for developing standard
operating procedures on how to manage various levels of aggression and
violence. Such procedures should detail how to manage violence, access
emergency medical treatment, make a police report and press charges, file
incident reports, and debrief staff involved with violent incidents.

A coordinated response plan and drills based on realistic scenarios add
to clinician safety. However, the most effective team response effort and
well-constructed protocol cannot negate one reality: the ultimate responsibility for safety remains with the individual clinician.

Education and Training

All clinicians should have mandatory, recurrent education about violence
safety during training, during early career years, and as a part of continuing
education throughout their careers. Formal presentations such as lectures
and seminars should address these topics:

Evaluation, differential diagnosis, and psychodynamics of violence. We should stress the importance of thorough history taking. Information obtained from outside sources is essential, particularly information about past violent behavior. Information about violent or sexual fantasies is important.

Standards and procedures for emergencies. Clinicians should understand use of communications, alarms such as panic buttons, restraint and seclusion protocols, and liability issues.

Consultation. In psychotherapy, pharmacotherapy, and group and milieu therapy, transference issues may lead to poor results and possibly unrecognized danger.

Education. Physicians should have additional education in psychopharmacology of aggressive and violent behavior, forensic issues of consent, involuntary commitment, treatment refusal, and duty to warn.

Training. Mandatory, recurrent education must include training in safety skills. These skills should be practiced in realistically simulated exercises under the supervision of qualified instructors. Training should be augmented with demonstration and audiovisual aids. Skills should include: de-escalating aggressive behavior, physical management of aggressive behavior, recognition of and response to dangerous situations, and basic self-defense techniques.

Reporting of Violence and Assaults

The high rate of violence and assault on mental health clinicians is a serious problem, yet studies indicate the number of assaults is underreported by a factor of five (Dubin and Lion, 1996). Accurate statistics play a crucial role in planning for increased clinician safety, and accuracy requires a uniform system of incident reporting. One difficulty in obtaining accurate statistics is the lack of uniformity in defining violence, assault, or aggression and the lack of uniform measures of severity. The following considerations could enhance clinician safety:

Identification of facilities or specific factors that result in higher assault and violence rates. These might include admission and/or staffing policies, better staff and security personnel training, and physical plant or protocol changes.

Identification of special categories of mental health clinicians at increased risk. These could include specialty area and work location and could include specific clinicians. Psychiatric residents and early-career psychiatrists, for example, are at increased risk.

Identification of certain behaviors or personality traits that may be predisposed to assault. Some personality factors, such as increased irritability in psychiatric residents, are associated with multiple assaults.

Identifying patient categories and individual patients with a greater likelihood of violence and assault. This could increase the effectiveness of flagging violence-prone patients to protect ward staff and individual clinicians better. It would greatly enhance epidemiological study of violence-prone individuals. It could underscore the significance of recidivism, as it is estimated that only 5 percent of patients cause 90 percent of violent assaults. Documentation of the most serious assaults, such as rape and homicide. Identification of the extent and severity of clinician danger. This would help overcome inertia among institutions, professional associations, and individuals in regard to addressing this extensive, extremely important problem.

Conclusions

Several factors contribute to inertia about clinician safety: Individual institutions do not want to be seen as having problems. Professional associations do not want to stigmatize mental health patients further, and they may give higher priority to other political concerns than the safety of their members. Individual clinicians may believe that violence and assault are part of the job or have feelings of guilt over such incidents. Always the overriding factor is a psychological denial of the fear of violence.

Recommendations

All clinicians should receive training on how to manage violent patients. Training review committees should be asked to consider the necessity for clinicians to be knowledgeable about violence.

Recertification examinations should include an assessment of clinicians' knowledge about managing violent patients.

Clinicians should be encouraged to collaborate with appropriate organizations concerning violent patients—prisons, jails, juvenile justice systems, probation offices, forensic hospitals, and community schools.

References

Baker, F. M., and Bell, C. C. "African-American Treatment Concerns." *Psychiatric Services*, 1999, *50*(3), 362–368.

Bass, J. N., and Beltis, J. "Therapeutic Effect of Fluoxetine on Naltrexone-Resistant Self-Injurious Behavior in an Adolescent with Mental Retardation." *Journal of Child and Adolescent Pharmacology*, 1991, *1*, 331–340.

Bell, C. C., Mock, L., and Slutkin, G. "The Need for Victimization Screening in Social Service Staff." *Journal of the National Medical Association*, forthcoming.

Bell, C. C., and Palmer, J. M. "Security Procedures in a Psychiatric Emergency Service." *Journal of the National Medical Association*, 1981, *73*(9), 835–842.

Berg, A. "Survival and the Ultimate Threat." *Psychiatric Times*, 1997, *14*(6), 33–36.

Brizer, D. A. "Introduction: Overview of Current Approaches to the Prediction of Violence." In D. A. Brizer and M. Crowner (eds.), *Current Approaches to the Prediction of Violence*. Washington D.C.: American Psychiatric Press, 1989.

Bureau of Justice Statistics. *Special Report: National Crime Victimization Survey, Workplace Violence, 1992–96.* NCJ 168634. Washington, D.C.: U.S. Department of Justice, Office of Justice Programs, July 1998.

Coccaro, E. F., Astill, J. L., Herbert, J. L., and Schut, A. G. "Fluoxetine Treatment of Impulsive Aggression in DSM-III-R Personality Disorder Patients." *Journal of Clinical Psychopharmacology,* 1990, *10*(5), 373–375.

Colling, R. L. *Basic Training Manual for Healthcare Security Officers.* Lombard, Ill.: International Association for Healthcare Security and Safety, 1995.

Colling, R. L. *Keeping the Healthcare Environment Safe.* Oakbrook Terrace, Ill.: Joint Commission on Accreditation of Healthcare Organizations, 1996.

De Becker, G. *The Gift of Fear: Survival Signals That Protect Us from Violence.* New York: Little, Brown, 1997.

Dubin, W. R., and Lion, J. R. "Violence Against the Medical Profession." In J. R. Lion, W. R. Dubin, and D. E. Futrell (eds.), *Creating a Secure Workplace.* Chicago: American Hospital Publishing, 1996.

Hare, R. D. *The Psychopathy Checklist—Revised.* Toronto: Multi-Health Systems, 1991.

Harris, G. T., and Rice, M. E. "Risk Appraisal and Management of Violent Behavior." *Psychiatric Services,* 1997, *48,* 1–9.

Hughes, D. H. "Acute Psychopharmacological Management of the Aggressive Psychotic Patient." *Psychiatric Services,* 1999, *50*(9), 1135–1137.

Krakowski, M. I., and Czobor, P. "Clinical Symptoms, Neurological Impairment, and Prediction of Violence in Psychiatric Inpatients." *Hospital and Community Psychiatry,* 1994, *45,* 700–705.

Ladds, B., and Lion, J. R. "Severe Assaults and Homicide Within Medical Institutions." In J. R. Lion, W. R. Dubin, and D. E. Futrell (eds.), *Creating a Secure Workplace.* Chicago: American Hospital Publishing, 1996.

Lion, J. R., Dubin, W. R., and Futrell, D. E. (eds.). *Creating a Secure Workplace.* Chicago: American Hospital Publishing, 1996.

Maier, G. J. "Training Security Staff in Aggression Management." In J. R. Lion, W. R. Dubin, and D. E. Futrell (eds.), *Creating a Secure Workplace.* Chicago: American Hospital Publishing, 1996.

Maier, G. J., Van Rybroek, G. J., and Mays, D. V. "A Report on Staff Injuries and Ambulatory Restraints: Dealing with Patient Aggression." *Journal of Psychosocial Nursing and Mental Health Services,* 1994, *32*(11), 23–29.

Marcovitz, E. "Aggression in Human Adaptation." *Psychoanalytic Quarterly,* 1973, *42,* 226–232.

Menninger, W. W. "Management of the Aggressive and Dangerous Patient." *Bulletin of the Menninger Clinic,* 1993, *57,* 208–217.

Mulvey, E. P. "Assessing the Evidence of a Link Between Mental Illness and Violence." *Hospital and Community Psychiatry,* 1994, *45,* 663–668.

Occupational Safety and Health Administration. *Guidelines for Preventing Workplace Violence for Health Care and Social Service Workers.* OSHA 3148. Washington, D.C.: U.S. Department of Labor, 1996.

Pynoos, R., and Nader, K. "Psychological First Aid for Children Who Witness Community Violence." *Journal of Traumatic Stress,* 1988, *1*(4), 445–473.

Reid, W. H., and Balis, G. U. "Evaluation of the Violent Patient." In R. E. Hales and A. J. Frances (eds.), *Psychiatric Update: The American Psychiatric Association Annual Review.* Vol. 6. Washington, D.C.: American Psychiatric Press, 1987.

Resnick, M. D., and others. "Protecting Adolescents from Harm: Findings from the National Longitudinal Study on Adolescent Health." *Journal of the American Medical Association,* 1997, *278*(10), 823–832.

Roy-Byrne, P. P., and Fann, J. R. "Psychopharmacologic Treatments for Patients with Neuropsychiatric Disorders." In S. C. Yudofsky and R. E. Hales (eds.), *The American*

Psychiatric Press Textbook of Neuropsychiatry. (3rd ed.) Washington, D.C.: American Psychiatric Press, 1997.

Saltzman, C., and others. "Parenteral Lorazepam Versus Parenteral Haloperidol for the Control of Psychiatric Disruptive Behavior." *Journal of Clinical Psychiatry,* 1991, *52,* 177–180.

Steadman, H. J., and others. "Violence by People Discharged from Acute Psychiatric Inpatient Facilities and by Others in the Same Neighborhoods." *Archives of General Psychiatry,* 1998, *55,* 393–401.

Swanson, J. W., Holzer, C. E., Ganju, V. K., and Jono, R. T. "Violence and Psychiatric Disorder in the Community: Evidence from the Epidemiologic Catchment Area Surveys." *Hospital and Community Psychiatry,* 1990, *41,* 761–770.

Tardiff, K. (ed.). *The Psychiatric Uses of Seclusion and Restraint.* Washington, D.C.: American Psychiatric Press, 1984.

Tardiff, K. "Determinants of Human Violence." In R. E. Hales and A. J. Frances (eds.), *Psychiatric Update: The American Psychiatric Association Annual Review.* Vol. 6. Washington, D.C.: American Psychiatric Press, 1987.

Tardiff, K. "Violence." In R. E. Hales, S. C. Yudofsky, and J. A. Talbott (eds.), *The American Psychiatric Press Textbook of Psychiatry.* (3rd ed.) Washington, D.C.: American Psychiatric Press, 1999.

Tohei, K. *This Is Aikido.* Tokyo: Japan Publications, 1975.

Tupin, J. P. "Usefulness of Lithium for Aggression." *American Journal of Psychiatry,* 1978, *135,* 1118.

Tupin, J. P. "The Violent Patient: A Strategy for Management and Diagnosis." *Hospital and Community Psychiatry,* 1983, *34,* 37–40.

U.S. Department of Health and Human Services. *Fatal Injuries to Workers in the United States, 1980–1989: A Decade of Surveillance.* Washington, D.C.: U.S. Department of Health and Human Services, Public Health Service, Centers for Disease Control and Prevention, National Institute for Occupational Safety and Health, 1993.

Walker, J. I. *Psychiatric Emergencies: Intervention and Resolution.* Philadelphia: Lippincott, 1983.

Westbrook, A., and Ratti, O. *Aikido and the Dynamic Sphere.* Rutland, Vt.: Charles E. Tuttle, 1974.

ARTHUR Z. BERG is assistant professor of psychiatry at Harvard Medical School and Massachusetts General Hospital. He is also a certified instructor in threat management and personal defense and a member of the American Society of Law Enforcement Trainers.

CARL C. BELL is professor of psychiatry and public health at the University of Illinois at Chicago and chief executive officer and president of the Community Mental Health Council and Foundation in Chicago.

JOE TUPIN is professor emeritus of psychiatry at the University of California, Davis, and medical director emeritus at the University of California, Davis, Medical Center.

3

In addition to taking steps to ensure their own safety, clinicians also have a role in predicting violence. In the past the clinician's ability to accurately assess the risk for violence has been seriously questioned. This chapter provides guidance for making acceptable predictions.

Assessing the Risk for Violence

Bradley R. Johnson

Because of psychiatrists' expertise in assessing behavior, we often request them to assess and predict future dangerousness of individuals in both clinical and forensic settings (see Chapter Two). Psychiatrists have different roles in predicting violence depending on the setting and the reason for the consultation. A psychiatrist may be requested, for example, to assess the apparent short-term violent behavior of a hospitalized, intensive care patient who is pulling out an intravenous line and threatening health staff. Alternatively, psychiatrists may need to assess the dangerousness of their own patients to determine their own duty to protect those who may be the target of patient violence (*Tarasoff v. The Regents of the University of California*, 1976). Finally, some psychiatrists are requested to predict long-term dangerousness in assessing an individual for civil commitment based on such standards as danger to self or danger to others.

Although studies on the predictability of future dangerousness conclude that psychiatrists overpredict potential violence, psychiatrists are better at assessing violence in acute situations or in patients who are suffering from acute psychiatric illnesses. Although there may be problems in predicting future violence with complete accuracy, when psychiatrists outline the risk factors for violence and understand what is currently happening with the patient, they are often able to predict violence in the short term with moderate accuracy.

An assessment of the risk for violence is a serious undertaking and should not be rushed. It may involve a prolonged clinical assessment and a thorough review of the individual's documented history from every possible source, including legal records and discussions with family, friends, witnesses, attorneys, and victims. Occasional use of screening instruments may be helpful in the clinical assessment.

The single best predictor of violence is a history of violence. It is vital that the evaluator assess whether the patient has suffered from singular or repetitive episodes of violence and whether they have been planned or impulsive. Assessment of the outcome of violent episodes (whether it leads to harm to others, harm to property, harm to oneself, or no physical or emotional harm) is important.

The development of violent tendencies is multidetermined and likely caused by a combination of biologically determined internal drives, learned socialization, and environmental stimuli. Although some individuals who suffer from mental illness become dangerous to themselves or others at times, most do not (see Chapter Two). Individuals suffering from organic neurological problems are frequently considered also at risk for violent outbursts (see Chapter One). Violence is often underpredicted in women. Gender is not a strong predictor of violence by the mentally ill (Binder, 1999).

The Study of Aggression

Violence is often considered physical aggression against other people, although some may consider verbal aggression toward others or physical aggression toward objects also to be forms of violence. These acts are considered criminal because the individual has violated the law. Due to the infrequent nature of violent episodes, the study of violence is difficult. Additionally, settings in which potentially aggressive individuals are located (jails, prisons, psychiatric state hospitals, and forensic units) do not easily lend themselves to research. Accordingly, violence studies are often based on biased populations; we have a great deal to learn.

The Clinical Evaluation

The psychiatric clinical evaluation is the starting point of any violence risk assessment. It is important to assess present and past psychiatric histories, medical history, social history, mental status, and the patient's past violent behavior. Because past violence is the single best predictor of future violence, asking questions regarding the extent of violent actions in the past and their frequency and type is paramount. Obtaining collateral information such as victims' accounts, family input, and other legal and medical records is helpful. One should look for patterns and similarities in the past violent acts. For example, does the individual act violently by himself or herself or in a family situation or both?

Because many violent acts happen while the individual is under the influence of alcohol or illicit substances, a detailed drug and alcohol history is required. Certain types of illicit drugs may diminish the ability to control behavior, and others may make the individual more paranoid or psychotic, increasing the chances of violent behavior. Because many lethal violent acts are secondary to the use of a gun, asking about gun ownership or other weapons and their current accessibility can be helpful in an acute case. Criminal histories and multiple psychiatric admissions may also increase the risk of an individual for future violent problems. Although not all violent perpetrators also commit sexual offenses, inquiry about a sexual aggression history is suggested.

The evaluator should pay attention to subjective feelings he or she experiences while evaluating an individual for future violence, although these can sometimes lead to overprediction if relied upon alone. Watching for specific themes such as lack of empathy, anger, threats to others, paranoia, and control can often signal a potential problem. Inquiring about various forms of violent fantasies can often be helpful. For individuals who suffer from comorbid psychiatric problems, gaining a detailed assessment of specific psychiatric risk factors is important (see Chapter Two).

The psychiatrist is often in a unique position to combine the psychology of behavior and medicine as part of the evaluation (see Chapter One). Assessing for seizures, head trauma, medical illnesses, and other neurological illnesses is important. Violent behavior has also been associated with dementia, exposure to certain chemical substances, metabolic disturbances, and even newly developed brain tumors. Regular physical examinations and routine laboratory tests can screen for most of these problems. Co-occurring antisocial personality disorder in patients with another psychiatric disorder may increase the likelihood of substance abuse, aggression, and violence. Finally, on occasion, violence has been associated with sexual disorders, homosexual panic, and even premenstrual syndrome.

Clinical Prediction

When assessing an individual for future violence, one must distinguish between a clinically oriented prediction and a statistically based one. A clinical prediction is based on an evaluator's skill, experience, and knowledge. A statistical prediction is an actuarial prediction based on statistical models and the use of risk factor instruments. In any setting an actuarial prediction is more accurate than a clinical prediction. However, because there is no universally accepted actuarial violence risk scale devised at this time, these do not stand alone in risk prediction and are used with the evaluator's impression, which is based on experience and solid psychiatric evaluation skills. Some evaluators like to use specific structured interviews or screening instruments. However, more important than the use of any specific evaluation tool is making sure that adequate clinical information is obtained no matter what the assessment method. Except in specific rare forensic cases, it is likely that most risk prediction can be done on an outpatient basis if adequate assessment time is allowed.

Risk Factors

Risk factors associated with violent behaviors come from biological, sociological, cognitive, and contextual sources. Biological risk factors may include such things as genetic predisposition, hormonal levels, perinatal complications, neurotoxins, or head injuries (see Chapter One). Socialization affects the way children learn rules, values, attitudes, and norms that guide behavior (see Chapter Four). Children learn by observing and modeling behaviors they see in society. Socialization risk factors include such things as teenage pregnancy, parents with a criminal history, parental rejection or abuse, and mentally ill parents. Other socialization risk factors may include such things as ownership of guns, exposure to media violence, drug and alcohol abuse, and gang membership. Cognitive factors include the notion that inadequate impulse or emotional control puts an individual at risk for violence only if violent acts are that person's preferred response learned through experiences. Such problems as mental retardation or severe learning disabilities may affect cognitive factors. Contextual risk factors may include such things as poverty, crowding, and deprivation. Socioeconomic inequality, not race, facilitates higher rates of violence among ethnic minority groups.

Screening Instruments

Instruments have been used in an attempt to assess aggression, anger, psychopathy, antisocial personality, and hostility and to predict violent recidivism. These instruments include but are not limited to

Minnesota Multiphasic Personality Inventory
Buss-Durkee Hostility Inventory
Monroe Episodic Dyscontrol Scale
Novaco Anger Scale
Hare Psychopathy Checklist–Revised
State-Trait Anger Expression Inventory
Brown-Goodwin Inventory
Albert Einstein College of Medicine Past Feelings and Acts of Violence Scale
Overt Aggressions Scale
Violence Risk Appraisal Guide

These screening instruments should not be used on their own to predict violent tendencies. They may be helpful to clarify or add information.

Legal and Ethical Issues

There are legal and ethical issues associated with violence risk prediction. First, when a patient has threatened danger to another identified person, most state courts have accepted the Tarasoff duty to protect ruling. However, there is often debate as to the degree that the psychiatrist may have to protect and under what specific circumstances. Tarasoff is also in conflict with the ethical standard of confidentiality, making it an exception to confidentiality. Second, informed consent is important in a violence risk assessment, including the fact that in a forensic case, what the evaluee says is likely to be placed in a report and used in multiple settings, again limiting the confidentiality that may be assumed.

Recommendations

Psychiatrists should not be afraid to use their expertise in assessing violence risk to the best of their ability based on modern-day knowledge and techniques. Although a few checklists and scales are used to aid in assessing or predicting violence and aggression, we should support research and grants for better testing of the validity of these instruments and for developing more predictive and actuarially derived rating tools. Additionally, more research to elicit knowledge of which specific psychiatric diagnoses are linked closely to violent behaviors and under which specific situations is encouraged. Finally, the use of thorough evaluations with review of multiple collateral sources as the current basis for risk prediction assessments is encouraged.

References

Binder, R. L. "Are the Mentally Ill Dangerous?" *Journal of the American Academy of Psychiatry and the Law,* 1999, 27, 189–201.

Tarasoff v. the Regents of the University of California, 131 CA 14, 551 P. 2d 334 (1976).

Additional Resources

Appelbaum, P. S., and Gutheil, T. G. *Clinical Handbook of Psychiatry and the Law.* Baltimore: Williams and Wilkins, 1991.

Dietz, P. E. "Patterns in Human Violence." In R. E. Hales, and A. J. Frances (eds.), *Psychiatric Update: The American Psychiatric Association Annual Review.* Vol. 6. Washington, D.C.: American Psychiatric Press, 1987.

Loeber, R., and Farrington, D. P. (eds.). *Serious and Violent Juvenile Offenders: Risk Factors and Successful Interventions.* Thousand Oaks, Calif.: Sage, 1998.

Monahan, J. *Predicting Violent Behavior: An Assessment of Clinical Techniques.* Thousand Oaks, Calif.: Sage, 1981.

Quinsey, V. L., Harris, G. T., Riu, M. G., and Cormier, C. A. *Violent Offenders: Appraising and Managing Risk.* Washington, D.C.: American Psychological Association, 1998.

Rosner, R. *Principles and Practice of Forensic Psychiatry.* New York: Chapman & Hall, 1994.

Segal, S. P., Watson, M. A., Goldfinger, S. M., and Averbuck, D. S. "Civil Commitment in the Psychiatric Emergency Room, I: The Assessment of Dangerousness by Emergency Room Clinicians." *Archives of General Psychiatry,* 1988, 45(8), 749–752.

Swanson, J. W. "Mental Disorder, Substance Abuse, and Community Violence: An Epidemiological Approach." In J. Mohahan and H. J. Steadman (eds.), *Violence in Mental Disorder: Developments in Risk Assessment.* Chicago: University of Chicago Press, 1994.

BRADLEY R. JOHNSON is a private practitioner and assistant professor at the University of Arizona College of Medicine, Department of Psychiatry. He is also the chief of psychiatry for the Arizona Community Protection and Treatment Center, where Arizona's civilly committed sexual offenders receive treatment.

4

Rebuilding the village, increasing access to health, improving bonding and attachment dynamics, providing opportunities to increase self-esteem and social skills enhancing the adult protective shield, and minimizing the impact of trauma are presented as basic principles to change health behavior. The intent of putting these principles into practice is to strengthen the two key support systems of children, the family and the school, so that they can provide primary prevention of violence.

Prevention of Violence

Carl C. Bell, Paul Jay Fink

The mental health profession has a moral and ethical role in assisting public health efforts to prevent violence. Accordingly, the prevention of abuse and victimization is part of the mission of the profession. Instituting child-rearing practices designed to improve and ensure bonding, attachment, and mastery best accomplishes the primary prevention of violence. To achieve this goal, mental health professionals must do systems work to increase resources for families. Furthermore, we should seek to minimize trauma and to eliminate corporal punishment as a societal norm. Our schools offer additional opportunities to develop infrastructure for supporting youth violence prevention efforts that will persist through adulthood. Secondary prevention activities require that we identify at-risk populations for perpetration and victimization and provide these people with a variety of services and support. Teaching children and adults techniques for seeking safety, resolving conflicts, and developing empathy are necessary components in this endeavor. Tertiary prevention focuses on helping those who have already perpetrated violence. The substructure to accomplish this goal should be developed in criminal justice and social services systems.

As individuals, mental health professionals must take a leadership role in the assessment and treatment of potential victims and perpetrators as well as become educators and advocates for the mental health profession and the public.

Scope of the Problem

Child abuse is a serious social problem in the United States (see Chapter Five). Approximately 2 million cases are reported annually, and approximately 1 million are confirmed. Child abuse homicide is one of the leading causes of childhood death, and every day a baby dies of abuse or neglect at the hands of caregivers. Every day 1,849 children are reported abused or neglected (National Research Council, 1993). Despite the recent accomplishments in youth and adult homicide reduction, there are still more than 24,000 youth homicides and spousal homicides per year. Youth violence and victimization continues to be a problem. Every day, 15 children are shot to death and 30 are wounded. Every four hours a child commits suicide. Though only 8 percent of the population, juveniles ages fourteen to twenty-four are responsible for 14 percent of all violent crimes, 50 percent of all murders, 25 percent of all property crimes, and a majority of all arson arrests. Children are the fastest-growing segment of the criminal population. Every four minutes a child is arrested for a violent crime; 30 percent of all crime is committed by juveniles. There are more than 200 million guns in the United States and more being manufactured and sold daily. The gun is the weapon used in the majority of murders in the United States, and every day 135,000 children take guns to school.

Prevention, Intervention, and Postvention

Bell, Flay, and Paikoff (forthcoming) propose seven key principles for changing health behavior: rebuilding the village; providing access to health care; improving bonding, attachment, and connectedness dynamics within the community and between stakeholders; improving self-esteem; increasing social skills; reestablishing the adult protective shield; and reducing the residual effects of trauma. These tenets brace the key support systems of children—the family and schools—in their efforts to prevent primary violence.

Rebuilding the Village

Communities with social fabric have less violence (Sampson, Raudenbush, and Earls, 1997). So it stands to reason that violence can be prevented by facilitating partnerships between community-based secular and nonsecular organizations. These partnerships could foster social infrastructure and community programmatic activities designed to reduce violent and disruptive behavior by and against youth in the schools and surrounding communities. The key to developing antiviolence programs in communities is improved communication, cooperation, coordination, and integration of agencies, both governmental and nongovernmental. Furthermore, engaging individuals to work toward improving the lot of young children by deterring them from violence is an important step. It requires advocacy and intelligent activism that brings together the scientific underpinnings of medicine, psychiatry, psychology, and sociology with a determination to help the community grow and provide safety for children. The best antidote for anger and violence is love and an unequivocal and positive approach to children by giving them the opportunity to gain self-respect and self-esteem.

Principals and faculty in schools who are willing to have outside agencies work together in the best interests of at-risk children will find that interventions are extremely beneficial. Jim Comer's work in New Haven, Connecticut, is a perfect example of this precept (Comer, 1980). Furthermore, from our work in Chicago and Philadelphia, we offer two models designed to rebuild the village.

By partnering with the religious community in the Interfaith Community Partnership, Chicago Public Schools (CPS) have increased attendance, improved school environments, provided positive role models, and created activities for youth. In this effort, CPS provides support to twelve religion-school-community partnership networks in each of the CPS regions. This partnership coordinates antiviolence marches with religious communities throughout the city. In addition, the network of secular and nonsecular organizations provides assistance in mentoring programs, off-site detention and community service programs, and assistance with after-school homework centers. Furthermore, there is a program that recruits men to escort children to and from school. During the Safe Schools, Safe Neighborhoods Summer 1998 initiatives, CPS partnered with the community by developing the CPS Youth Outreach Workers program. This initiative trained one hundred violence-intervention specialists, including off-duty police officers, community members, parents, teachers, and social workers, to provide alternative activities for youth in high-crime areas. Also, a newly created referral service network provided follow-up services for more than two thousand referrals for suicidal ideation, recreational activities, job preparation, job orientation, job placement, gang detachment, and housing relocation. In addition, CPS youth outreach workers' efforts helped with collaborative partnerships with more than fifty governmental and city agencies and community-based organizations. CPS has developed many school-community activities, especially for schools whose communities experience high rates of violence.

In Philadelphia, a cluster of twelve schools holds two meetings a month at the city's middle schools. In attendance are the counselors from the feeder elementary schools and the high schools and outside agencies such as the department of human services, the probation department, and community mental health centers. At these meetings the group focuses on individual students and works on a school plan so that the child and child's family will receive needed services. Essentially, a village is rebuilt around the child and the child's family. Various agencies provide information about the child and his or her family along with services to help solve identified problems. This effort replaces the punitive attitude found in some school districts with efforts to identify at-risk children, help them reduce precursors to violent and disruptive behavior, and foster cooperative programs between schools and other appropriate agencies of all types. We need to realize that decisions made in the best interests of children will, over time, change the state of the community.

Providing Access to Health Care

Evidence suggests that children with high exposure to lead may be predisposed to violence (Earls, 1991). Furthermore, there is evidence that children with attention deficit hyperactivity disorder (ADHD) may be predisposed to violence and conduct disorder (Kline and others, 1977). ADHD may also predispose children to engaging in other high-risk behaviors such as drug abuse or early sexual activity (American Psychiatric Association, 1994). There is additional evidence that neuropsychiatric disorders may predispose individuals to violence (Lewis and others, 1985; Moffitt, 1997). Clearly, treatment for psychiatric or behavioral disorders that predispose individuals to engage in high-risk behaviors is essential to promote violence prevention in those afflicted individuals.

As interpersonal violence is exacerbated by substance abuse, early intervention in substance abuse may prevent subsequent violence. Getting parents to cooperate is a complex part of addressing the needs of children; having clinics in the schools not only makes it easier for the child but sensitizes the entire faculty to the value of psychiatric intervention (Comer, 1980). However, trying to deal with substance abuse in the schools and identifying kids who are abusing substances is difficult for schools, as the issue of punishment versus treatment often becomes confounded.

Addressing the mental health needs of children in juvenile detention calls for another systemic approach to helping violent-prone youth with psychiatric and substance abuse problems. Unfortunately, juvenile detention institutions often complicate the care of the mentally ill child and may create new problems for children who have to adjust to a much more complex, meaner, and less empathic environment than the school. The child's reaction is usually alienation and indifference. This is not to say that children who commit crimes shouldn't be punished. However, every effort should be made to examine and evaluate the needs of each child and to address the child in a nonpunitive way to allow for discovery about the causes and nature of the child's behavior. The Philadelphia Youth Homicide Committee has found that a significant number of kids who become victims or perpetrators of homicide had previously spent time incarcerated with no positive effects. Research is needed to discover why some children succeed and others fail in programs that are structured and offer reasonably good personnel and service delivery.

Improving Bonding, Attachment, and Connectedness

Some of the roots of youth and adult violence are believed to be planted in the early experience of child abuse. Interventions to prevent child abuse are proving to be extremely powerful and effective and may be a critical form of violence prevention. In Hawaii, the Healthy Start program has reduced child abuse by 80 percent. In addition, nursing home visitation has been shown to be effective in preventing child abuse (Olds and others, 1997). These interventions identify potentially abusive pregnant women and provide them with supportive services designed to help them bond with their children. Likewise, it is important for preschool children to grow up in supportive, nurturing environments; thus support for preschool programs (for children ages zero to five) is essential in prevention.

In schools it is possible to reduce violence by helping the school system emphasize activities designed to increase students' attachment to their families, to one another, and to their school (Gorman-Smith and others, 1996; Pinderhughes, 1972, 1979; Resnick and others, 1997). Expanding the school day and school year to provide structured academic and recreational activities for children, including a nutritious dinner meal, will increase attachment to the schools. Connectedness to schools can also be accomplished by helping schools provide educational opportunities for infants, toddlers, preschoolers, and their parents so children are better prepared for life. Programs such as Zero to Three, Head Start, nursing home visitation, and Healthy Start can all be supported by public schools (Bell, Gamm, Vallas, and Jackson, forthcoming). Juvenile delinquency can be reduced through the development of adequate after-school activities and adequate supervision and by keeping the school buildings open so they can serve as community centers and refuges. The use of school uniforms might also improve a student's sense of school connectedness.

Increased student attendance, reduction in truancy, and a reduction in the drop-out rate would also likely decrease violence by keeping children off the streets and out of destructive systems. In Philadelphia, truancy has been found to be the earliest marker in children who are murdered or who become murderers: a significant number of these children were truant a great deal and in the final years of their schooling missed 60 to 80 percent of the school year, leading them to drop out of school (Paul Jay Fink, personal communication, Youth Homicide Committee, 1999). As a result of this finding, truancy court in Philadelphia was decentralized into the schools, allowing ten thousand hearings per year instead of two thousand. Because of this restructuring, there have been four thousand more children in school every day in the 1998–1999 school year than in the 1997–1998 school year. In addition, the police picked children up from the streets during school hours and took them to the nearest school. By expanding the number of truancy court appearances, Philadelphia was able to lower the threshold from 50 absent days to 25 absent days. Furthermore, bringing truancy court into the schools allowed school personnel to be present at the hearings to give information about the problem.

The Philadelphia Youth Homicide Committee (1999) also has determined that a lot of children who had trouble in the ninth grade dropped out in the tenth grade. Accordingly, they propose giving attention to children who are making the transition from middle school to high school. To do a more complete job of making school a compatible place, we also have to look at the number of suspensions and the transition from eighth to ninth grades.

Increasing Self-Esteem

Self-esteem comes from feeling competent to do what must be done, acknowledging and respecting the qualities and characteristics about oneself that are special and different, having models that can be used to make sense of the world, and feeling a sense of satisfaction from being connected to people, places, or things (Bean, 1992). If we propose to change health behavior, improving target recipients' self-esteem is a critical component in any successful prevention and intervention strategy (Bell, Flay, and Paikoff, forthcoming). Bell (1997) suggests that constructive activities help youth develop social skills and self-esteem that reduce engagement in risky behaviors. This can be accomplished by incorporating high school service-learning requirements in the curriculum and training on how youth may avoid or prevent violence (for example, values and character education, social skills training, and conflict resolution training). Providing youth with opportunities to serve their community, resolve disputes peacefully, and develop leadership skills that will enable them to model and promote healthy alternatives to violence is also effective. Mentoring is also a valuable method for introducing positive modeling and unconditional love.

Increasing Social Skills

Parenting education, nonviolent disciplinary practices, conflict resolution, leadership, anger management, classroom behavior management, and openness to learning are all social skills that have the potential for preventing violence.

Family: Parenting Education and Early Intervention. Expanding child-care resources to help young, inexperienced parents raise children and carry out their parental roles in a loving, caring way will provide safety for the child. Borduin and others (1985) note that improving intrafamily relations—closeness, positive statements, communication clarity, and emotional cohesion—can reduce risk for serious antisocial behavior and violence. Low levels of parental warmth, acceptance, and affection and low levels of cohesion and high levels of conflict and hostilities have been associated with delinquent and violent behavior (Farrington, 1989; Henggeler, Melton, and Smith, 1992; Tolan and Lorion, 1988). Aggressive children show more "insecure" attachment styles, and delinquency and weak attachment bonds to parents are associated (Booth, Spieker, Barnard, and Morisset, 1992). The reduction and elimination of physical, emotional, and sexual abuse of children is vital if we are to reduce violence in our society through primary prevention.

Straus (1991) notes that there is widespread acceptance of corporal punishment for children. Furthermore, there is significant negative fallout from corporal punishment, as all corporal punishment has the effect of causing children to be confused and ambivalent about the people they love: they are filled with anger, hatred, and resentment at being dealt with in such a negative way. When children are hit in adolescence, the humiliation is devastating, and their struggle to develop their personal identity and autonomy may be set back and seriously damaged. Teaching parents how to use effective punishments such as time-outs and small deprivations as well as how to talk to their children would be an excellent substitute for the impulse to hit and hurt children. Identification with one's aggressor is common, and people usually raise their children the way they were raised—unless they work very hard to counter the automatic, unconscious tendency to do unto others according to their conditioning. Therefore, a general rule to eliminate corporal punishment can have a strong effect on parents' being more creative and finding new ways to deal with issues of negative behavior by children.

Schools.   Weissberg and Elias (1993) and Weissberg and Greenberg (1997) have long been proponents of teaching social skills as tools to help youth avoid risky behaviors. Schools are in an outstanding position to help school staff and parents improve their ability to teach children appropriate social skills and to use positive interventions to decrease disruptive student behavior. In addition, social skills are created via the very process of school education.

Social skills can be enhanced by giving youth opportunities to serve their community, resolve disputes peacefully, and develop leadership skills. For example, CPS is providing opportunities for youth to be involved with a teen court program and a peer leaders program in which students teach students peer mediation, conflict resolution, and anger management skills. The CPS Young Negotiators program teaches student negotiation skills, and in the Peer Mediation program students learn from peers to manage conflict and disagreements using a diversity of techniques that allow them to avoid violence and other forms of aggressive and antisocial behavior. Finally, by being involved in mentoring programs and service clubs, youth learn additional social skills. Teams of people with special knowledge in shaping school climates can help in the development of safety plans to be included in school improvement plans. The Boys Town Educational Model offers a social and life skills curriculum training model that provides intervention strategies to school personnel. Furthermore, behavior management training programs can provide techniques to modify students' disruptive and aggressive behavior and to help students maintain self-control and engage in socially proactive behavior (Bell, Gamm, Vallas, and Jackson, forthcoming).

Improving the process of education can also increase social skills. This can be accomplished by

Improving the academic performance of all students by requiring students (including those with disabilities and limited-English proficiency), teachers, administrators, and schools to be accountable
Providing learning outcome standards and relevant staff development
Developing lesson plans consistent with the standards and making them available to teachers

Establishing a rigorous high school core curriculum junior and senior high school academies

Expanding the International Baccalaureate programs to high schools

Establishing regional high schools with academic entrance criteria

Collaborating with area colleges and universities to provide college courses for motivated and able students

Providing individualized strategies for children having academic difficulty

Providing tutoring services

Establishing smaller class sizes and special curricula for retained students

Establishing transition centers for retained students of high school age

Implementing a capital development program

First Steps, a program from the Oregon Social Learning Center, diverts preschool children who show early signs of bullying or other aggressive behavior from a path leading to delinquency and violence. Working both at school and at home, the program takes thirty days at school and six weeks of in-home parent training. In First Steps the little preschooler, typically a boy aged four to six who is known for bullying his classmates, can be taught how to take turns, how to ask before taking what he wants, how to wait in line without pushing or shoving, and how to get attention in constructive ways. This is a very structured, reward-based collaboration between parents and the classroom, which, done at this early age, appears to break aggressive patterns for more than half of the First Step pupils continuing into grade school.

Reestablish the Adult Protective Shield

As it is clear that children can be identified as having problems and needing help as early as first grade, it is possible to identify children at risk. The statistics gathered on youth murder victims and perpetrators in Philadelphia in 1995 showed that 80 percent of the perpetrators and 52 percent of the decedents had their first arrest between the ages of ten and fourteen. If they were arrested at ten, it is clear that they were probably disturbed and causing great havoc at age seven or eight. Thus it is important for us not to think that violence begins when the child reaches adolescence. Rather, it is critical that we find ways to help families and children by recognizing the disturbed child as early as possible, evaluating that child, and insisting that some community action be taken to deal appropriately with the problem.

Helping to reestablish the adult protective (Pynoos and Nader, 1988) shield is another violence-prevention strategy. This can be accomplished by implementing safety through the use of parent patrols, enhanced training and expansion of security personnel, rapid response teams of school security and city police department staff, after-school security patrols, informational booklets for parents on the safe passage of students to and from school, metal detectors in every middle and high school, and surveillance cameras (Bell,

Gamm, Vallas, and Jackson, forthcoming). To a great extent, the "Boston miracle" of the 1990s, when the youth homicide rate dropped dramatically, involved this principle of reestablishing the adult protective shield. Simply put, monitored behavior is less likely to be antisocial than is unmonitored behavior.

The media promulgate violence, and this has had a significant effect on societal values and norms over the last fifty years. The adult protective shield could also be reestablished by reducing inappropriate, gratuitous, and repetitive violence in the media.

Reducing the Residual Effects of Trauma

The final violence prevention strategy is to minimize the residual effects of victimization (see Chapter Eight). The Yale Department of Psychiatry Public Health/Mental Health Partnership Model is a good example of a cooperative effort between police and mental health officials to address the problems of children who witness traumatic events (Marans and others, 1995).

Mental health professionals must pledge themselves to reducing traumatic stress in our society, whether it is the stress of abuse or the incredible traumas related to distortions in family life, disruption of families through divorce and death, and other such events. There is clear evidence that witnessing trauma causes real changes in the brain (see Chapter Eight). Some children are naturally resilient or have the tools that allow them to resist the downward pull of traumatic events (Bell and Suggs, 1998). Whether it is through the unconditional love of someone in their lives or whether it is an inborn biological or genetic capability, it is an important factor. In addition the trauma of corporal punishment must be reduced and corporal punishment abandoned as a means of disciplining children.

Recommendations

We recommend that mental health professionals get training in violence prevention principles, community activism, and developing school-based programs. Our profession needs to understand and embrace its public health role. Helping change public policy so that schools can use mental health professionals for early identification of and intervention with potentially violent children would be a valuable step.

Considering the new brain research, enhancing research about the causes, effects, and sequelae of violence and trauma is an important part of future violence prevention efforts. It is possible that this new century will see the development of specific medications that will help curb some sources of excessive temper (see Chapter One). However, without developing proper infrastructure in settings where such patients are likely to be found (such as in corrections), our violence prevention efforts will be applied where they are least needed.

References

American Psychiatric Association. *Diagnostic and Statistical Manual of Mental Disorders: Fourth Edition*. Washington, D.C.: American Psychiatric Press, 1994.

Bean, R. *The Four Conditions of Self-Esteem: A New Approach for Elementary and Middle Schools*. (2nd ed.) Santa Cruz, Calif.: ETR Associated, 1992.

Bell, C. C. "Promotion of Mental Health Through Coaching of Competitive Sports." *Journal of the National Medical Association*, 1997, *89*(8), 517–520.

Bell, C. C., Flay, B., and Paikoff, R. "Strategies for Health Behavioral Change." In J. Chunn (ed.), *Health Behavioral Change Imperative*, forthcoming.

Bell, C. C., Gamm, S., Vallas, P., and Jackson, P. "Strategies for the Prevention of Youth Violence in Chicago Public Schools." In M. Shafii and S. Shafii (eds.), *School Violence: Contributing Factors, Management, and Prevention*. Washington, D.C.: American Psychiatric Press, forthcoming.

Bell, C. C., and Suggs, H. "Training Heart: Using Sports to Create Resiliency in Children." *Child and Adolescent Psychiatric Clinics of North America*, 1998, *4*, 859–865.

Booth, C. L., Spieker, S. J., Barnard, K. E., and Morisset, C. E. "Infants at Risk: The Role of Preventive Intervention in Deflecting a Maladaptive Developmental Trajectory." In J. McCord and R. E. Tremblay (eds.), *Preventing Antisocial Behavior: Interventions from Birth Through Adolescence*. New York: Guilford Press, 1992.

Borduin, C., and others. *Changed Lives: The Effects of the Perry School Preschool on Youths Through Age 19*. Ypsilanti, Mich.: High Scope Press, 1985.

Comer, J. *School Power: Implications of an Intervention Project*. New York: Free Press, 1980.

Earls, F. "A Developmental Approach to Understanding and Controlling Violence." In H. E. Fitzgerald (ed.), *Theory and Research in Behavioral Pediatrics*. Vol. 5. New York: Plenum Press, 1991.

Farrington, D. P. "Early Predictors of Adolescent Aggression and Adult Violence." *Violence and Victims*, 1989, *4*, 79–100.

Gorman-Smith, D., and others. "The Relation of Family Functioning to Violence Among Inner-City Minority Youths." *Journal of Family Psychology*, 1996, *10*, 115–129.

Henggeler, S. W., Melton, G. B., and Smith, L. A. "Family Preservation Using Multisystemic Therapy: An Effective Alternative to Incarcerating Serious Juvenile Offenders." *Journal of Consultation Clinical Psychology*, 1992, *60*, 953–961.

Kline, R. G., and others. "Clinical Efficacy of Methylphenidate in Conduct Disorder with and Without Attention Deficit Hyperactivity Disorder." *Archives of General Psychiatry*, 1997, *54*, 1073–1080.

Lewis, D. O., and others. "Biosocial Characteristics of Children Who Later Murder: A Prospective Study." *American Journal of Psychiatry*, 1985, *142*, 1161–1167.

Marans, S., and others. *The Police-Mental Health Partnership*. New Haven, Conn.: Yale University Press, 1995.

Moffitt, T. E. "Neuropsychology, Antisocial Behavior, and Neighborhood Context." In J. McCord (ed.), *Violence and Childhood in the Inner City*. New York: Cambridge University Press, 1997.

National Research Council. *Understanding Child Abuse and Neglect*. Washington, D.C.: National Academy Press, 1993.

Olds, D. L., and others. "Long-Term Effects of Home Visitation on Maternal Life Course and Child Abuse and Neglect: Fifteen-Year Follow-Up of a Randomized Trial." *Journal of the American Medical Association*, 1997, *278*, 637–643.

Pinderhughes, C. A. "Managing Paranoia in Violent Relationships." In G. Usdin (ed.), *Perspectives on Violence*. New York: Brunner/Mazel, 1972.

Pinderhughes, C. A. "Differential Bonding: Toward a Psychophysiological Theory of Stereotyping." *American Journal of Psychiatry*, 1979, *136*, 33–37.

Pynoos, R., and Nader K. "Psychological First Aid for Children Who Witness Community Violence." *Journal of Traumatic Stress*, 1988, *1*(4), 445–473.

Resnick, M. D., and others. "Protecting Adolescents from Harm—Findings from the National Longitudinal Study on Adolescent Health." *Journal of the American Medical Association,* 1997, *278*(10), 823–832.

Sampson, R. J., Raudenbush, S. W., and Earls, F. "Neighborhoods and Violent Crime: A Multilevel Study of Collective Efficacy." *Science,* 1997, *277,* 918–924.

Straus, M. A. *Beating the Devil Out of Them: Corporal Punishment in American Families.* San Francisco: New Lexington Press, 1991.

Tolan, P. H., and Lorion, R. P. "Multivariate Approaches to the Identification of Delinquency Proneness in Males." *American Journal of Community Psychology,* 1988, *16,* 547–561.

Weissberg, R. P., and Elias, M. J. "Enhancing Young People's Social Competence and Health Behavior." *Applied and Preventive Psychology,* 1993, *3,* 179–190.

Weissberg, R. P., and Greenberg, T. "School and Community Competence Enhancement and Prevention Programs." In E. Sigel and K. A. Renninger (eds.), *Handbook of Child Psychology.* Vol. 4: *Child Psychology in Practice.* (5th ed.) New York: Wiley, 1997.

CARL C. BELL is professor of psychiatry and public health at the University of Illinois at Chicago and chief executive officer and president of the Community Mental Health Council and Foundation in Chicago.

PAUL JAY FINK is professor of psychiatry at the Temple University School of Medicine; senior consultant at the Charter Behavioral Health System; and past president of the American Psychiatric Association.

5

*Domestic and intimate partner abuse, child and adoles-
cent physical and sexual abuse, and elder abuse constitute
family violence. Such violence is responsible for a significant proportion of intentional injury and, accordingly, is a
major public health problem. This chapter provides information on aspects of each type of family violence.*

Family Violence

Sandra J. Kaplan

Family violence, which includes domestic and intimate partner abuse, child
and adolescent physical and sexual abuse and neglect, and elder abuse, is a
major public health problem. Domestic and intimate partner abuse is the
leading cause of injury to women. Almost two million women are severely
assaulted by their partners each year, with domestic violence involving 20
percent of U.S. couples. The incidence of child abuse has increased. Approximately six out of every one thousand children and adolescents are recognized as physically abused as a direct result of child maltreatment. Fifteen
hundred die and three in every one thousand children and adolescents are
recognized as sexually abused each year. Elder abuse is estimated to affect
up to 10 percent of those over sixty-five years of age.

Domestic and intimate partner abuse is increasingly a priority of health,
law enforcement, judicial, and legislative initiatives. Currently, all fifty states
have mandatory child abuse and mandatory or voluntary elder abuse reporting laws. However, there is still an urgent need for additional attention and
resources.

Although family violence affects all racial, ethnic, religious, and socioeconomic groups, poverty increases risk. Family violence is usually a recurrent phenomenon that escalates in severity and frequency and affects the communities,
future generations, and significant others of those exposed to it as children.
Exposure to family violence also increases the risk for behavioral and emotional
problems and the impairment of vocational, social, and academic functioning.
Exposure to family violence is associated with increased rates of suicide, homicide, conduct disorder, depression, childhood separation anxiety, posttraumatic
stress disorder (PTSD), alcohol and drug abuse, and cigarette smoking. In addition, those exposed often suffer from impaired self-esteem and feelings of hopelessness and helplessness.

Risk factors for violence in the family include the following:

Victim-perpetrator power imbalance with the target often being smaller, younger, or more frail than the perpetrator
Perpetrator and target depressive and substance abuse disorders
Females as the targets of anger
Stressful family events
Four or more children closely spaced
Young or single parenthood
Social isolation
Childhood exposure to family violence

Mental health assessment and treatment of victims, witnesses, and perpetrators of family violence and agency consultations by mental health professionals (MHPs) have been found to be effective in the cessation of this violence and in the rehabilitation of family members. Increases in legislative, judicial, and law enforcement advocacy have also been effective in preventing family violence. Considering the good outcomes of intervention, advocacy for comprehensive biopsychosocial assessments and service plans for family violence victims, perpetrators, and witnesses need to become more vigorous. Formulation and implementation of protocols for the identification of all types of family violence need to become more arduous. MHPs also need to increase their knowledge of applicable laws concerning reporting and protection of targets, witnesses, and perpetrators of all types of family violence. It is essential that mental health trade associations use their resources to provide assessment, protection, and treatment interventions for families with violence. These organizations also need to participate with local, state, and national government and advocacy agencies that support advocacy for increased resources and finances for the prevention, recognition, protection, and treatment of families with violence. In addition, increased participation in multidisciplinary research efforts to identify the mental health effects and service needs of those exposed to and perpetrating family violence is also urgently needed. Finally, the provision of family violence prevention, identification, rehabilitation, and education is essential for all mental health professionals during and after their specialty training.

Domestic and Intimate Partner Abuse

Domestic violence refers to the injury of adults or adolescents by their significant (and intimate) others regardless of their marital status, living arrangements, or sexual orientation. It is an ongoing, debilitating experience of physical, psychological, and/or sexual abuse in the home, associated with increased isolation from the outside world and limited personal freedom and accessibility to resources. It includes pushing, shoving, slapping, punching, kicking, and choking; assault with a weapon; holding, tying down, or restraining; and refusing help when sick or injured. Emotional or psychological abuse may precede or accompany physical violence as a means of controlling through fear or degradation. It may include the following: threats of harm, physical and social isolation, extreme jealousy and possessiveness, deprivation, intimidation, degradation, humiliation, and financial control. Sexual abuse in violent intimate partner relationships may include any form of forced sex or sexual degradation such as trying to make a partner perform sexual acts against his or her will, pursuing sexual activity when a partner is not fully conscious or has not consented, hurting the partner physically during sex or assaulting his or her genitals, and coercing partners to have sex without protection against pregnancy or sexually transmitted disease.

Prevalence. Domestic violence is the leading cause of injury to women: 1.8 million U.S. women are severely assaulted by their partners each year. It has been estimated to occur among 16 to 25 percent of U.S. couples, with injury to women more likely than to men. Marital rape is prevalent, and 36 percent of battered women report having been raped by their husbands or cohabiting partners.

Risk Factors and Effects. The risk factors for domestic violence include victim-perpetrator power imbalance, with the highest prevalence rates found in male-dominated dyads and the lowest prevalence in egalitarian spousal dyads. Substance abuse and depression are risk factors for and also probably effects of domestic violence. Although domestic violence occurs in all socioeconomic classes, socioeconomic disadvantage increases risk. Economic dependency of victims is often present. The outcome of domestic violence on victims includes constant terror and anxiety with fears of imminent doom, inability to relax or sleep and violent nightmares when the person does sleep, stress-related disorders such as PTSD, passivity and lack of energy, depression and suicidal behavior, a sense of being hopeless and powerless, and substance abuse (see Chapter Eight). Children who witness domestic violence often have difficulties with various stress-related disorders such as separation anxiety or PTSD, aggressive behavior toward siblings and peers, temper tantrums, stealing and truancy, depression, learning problems, somatic symptoms, enuresis, insomnia, impaired concentration, difficulty with schoolwork, poor social competence, substance abuse, and cigarette use.

Best Practices. Recognition and diagnosis of domestic and intimate partner abuse and collaboration with legal and community resources to ensure protection of the victims is the first course of action. Training emergency room staff in domestic violence recognition leads to an increased number of patients correctly diagnosed as having traumatic injuries from domestic violence assaults. Efforts should also be made to increase facilities and resources for treatment of the physical and psychological injuries of the victims, witnesses, and perpetrators of family violence. Furthermore, we need more advocacy to increase prevention and research. The role of MHPs is multifaceted and depends on the place (emergency room, inpatient facility, outpatient office, or courtroom) and time of the intervention (immediately after the violence, intermediate periods between violent episodes, or during separation). Additionally, the clinician will need to network with social services, police, domestic violence advocacy groups, and the legal system to plan a coordinated therapeutic intervention, often involving judicial orders of protection, law enforcement, and domestic violence advocacy agencies.

Treatment must first consider protection of the assaulted partner from both further assault and from suicide risk, particularly during the acute period. The cessation of the battering is the immediate concern. A long-term therapeutic goal is to facilitate the assaulted partner's independence by treating any assault-related psychological symptoms. Interdisciplinary teams; outreach; twenty-four-hour, on-call coverage; and evening hours make it possible to rehabilitate persons in violent families. Useful services include

Mental health and substance abuse evaluation and treatment (including individual, group, and family therapy for parents and children)
Assessment and remediation of child educational and adult vocational status
Training in social skills, parenting, and nonviolent conflict resolution
Financial, housing, and homemaking assistance referral capacity
Legal advocacy

Treatment.   Crisis intervention in domestic and intimate partner abuse is aimed at protecting the victim and teaching him or her about safety risks and how to resolve possible future crises by applying crisis resolution techniques. Individual psychotherapy seeks to clarify the ambivalent feelings of the battered partner to the batterer and to continue protection against violence. Couple and family therapy with individual and conjoint sessions should take place only after individual treatments for the victim and the batterer have ensured the safety of the victim. Individual and conjoint sessions may also focus on anger and self-control skills as well as assertive behavior. A major goal of treatment may be to empower victims to separate from violent partners by strengthening their independence and self-esteem. To be self-sufficient, the victim may also need vocational counseling and self-help groups. Given the impact of witnessing domestic violence on children, parenting therapy and child therapy may be necessary to assist the rehabilitation of all members of families with children. In an effort to address the sequelae of domestic violence, treatment for substance abuse; depression, including suicide risk assessment; stress-related disorders; and physical injuries, including neurological injuries, may be needed. Monitoring of ongoing progress and case management with involved agencies is also needed.

Arrest and other law enforcement and judicial efforts are critical tools in engaging violent partners in rehabilitation. Behavioral treatments focusing on the battering partner's problems with anger control and substance abuse treatment may be indicated. It may also be important to get a neuropsychiatric consultation for batterers (see Chapters One and Two). Treatment programs for batterers are becoming more common, and their usage as referral programs by civil and criminal courts is growing more widespread.

Research. Psychiatric research and demonstration projects need to be designed for the prevention of partner abuse. Different dynamics and consequences of abuse for men and women and the service implications of these differences have to be identified.

Advocacy. Prevention programs will be enhanced by advocating for control of firearms. Furthermore, there is a need to collaborate with the media to control public violence exposure. Another important advocacy goal is promoting programs that teach empathy and provide nurturing role models and nonviolent conflict resolution. It is equally important to enhance the value of those most likely to be victims of domestic violence: women and the elderly. Advocacy by MHPs for community collaboration and education will contribute to the prevention of domestic violence. This education should begin in elementary school as an essential part of health education for all children and should continue as a component of health education throughout the life span (see Chapter Four).

Child and Adolescent Physical, Sexual, and Emotional Abuse and Physical and Emotional Neglect

Child and adolescent physical abuse is defined as present when a child under age eighteen has experienced injury (harm standard) or risk of injury (endangerment standard) as a result of having been hit with a hand, stick, strap, or other object or having been punched, kicked, shaken, thrown, burned, stabbed, or choked by a parent or parent substitute. Child and adolescent sexual abuse involves a child under eighteen years of age having experienced one or more of the following types of sexual acts: intrusion defined as evidence of oral, anal, or genital penile penetration or anal or genital digital or other penetration; molestation with genital contact, but without evidence of intrusion; acts that involve contact with nongenital areas of a child's body (such as fondling of breasts or buttocks); or inadequate or inappropriate supervision resulting in sexual activities with the perpetrator—parent, parent substitute, or some other person. In addition, child sexual abuse may take the forms of exposure (viewing of sexual acts, pornography, and exhibitionism), molestation (fondling of either the child's or the adult's genitals), sexual intercourse, and rape. Physical neglect refers to harm or endangerment as a result of inadequate nutrition, clothing, hygiene, and supervision. Emotional abuse includes verbal abuse, harsh nonphysical punishments (such as being tied up), and threats of maltreatment, and emotional neglect includes failure to provide adequate affection and emotional support and permitting a child to be exposed to domestic violence.

Epidemiology. In 1993, the Third National Incidence Study found that almost six per one thousand children were physically abused, three per one thousand children were sexually abused, and eight per one thousand children were neglected. Fifteen hundred abuse fatalities of children were reported in 1993. In 1997, the National Child Abuse and Neglect Data System compiled from state child protective service agencies found that physical abuse involved 25 percent, sexual abuse involved 12 percent, and neglect more than 50 percent of all child maltreatment cases. The most frequent reporters of maltreatment, in descending order, were educators, law enforcement officers, social services personnel, and health providers (with psychiatrists being the lowest reporters of abuse). During 1997, 67 percent of child maltreatment victims were white, 30 percent were African American, 13 percent were Hispanic, 3 percent were Native American, and 1 percent were Asian or Pacific Islander.

Risk factors for physical abuse and neglect include the risk factors for family violence and also parental substance abuse, parental depression, and child disability (mental, physical, or cognitive).

The majority of sexually abused children are girls (77 percent), although a significant number of boys are also abused. Boy victims tend to be younger and more severely abused and over longer periods of time. Most of the perpetrators are men, and abuse may occur as one incident, as occasional incidents, or as a gradually escalating level of maltreatment. At the time of the abuse it may not be experienced as aversive by the child; only in adolescence is it recognized as sexual abuse. Many sexually abused children are under pressure by the perpetrator not to tell. There may be threats that the perpetrator will commit suicide or harm the child or that there will be family dissolution or that the child will be taken away from the home and put into foster care.

The risk factors for sexual abuse are

The child is the first born
The child is female
One of the child's parents is absent
There is a step family
There is a chaotic family life
The perpetrator uses alcohol or drugs
The perpetrator has marital or sexual dissatisfaction
The perpetrator was exposed in childhood to personal or witnessed familial child sexual abuse

Effects of Physical and Sexual Abuse and Neglect Found in Persons Under Eighteen.   Additional discussion of the impact of victimization can be found in Chapters Six and Seven. In general, the effects of physical and sexual abuse and neglect in children may include

Major depressive, dysthymic, and conduct disorders
Drug abuse and cigarette smoking
Affect dysregulation, including difficulty controlling anger or blunted affect
Negative social interactions with peers and social isolation
Insecure attachment
Frontotemporal and anterior region EEG abnormalities
Impaired self-concept
Impaired sleep efficiency
Increased risk for suicidal thoughts and behaviors (particularly associated
    with sexual abuse)
PTSD
Dissociative disorders
Eating disorders
Sexualized behavior and attitudes
Premature onset of menses in females

All types of child maltreatment have been associated with delays in physical growth and learning and academic problems.

Best Practices. Sexual abuse preventive methods include prosecution and treatment of offenders. Furthermore, preventive educational programs that teach children about their bodies and the nature and appropriateness of different relationships can inform them of their rights and self-worth and provide them with the skills to avoid sexual abuse and to report actual or potential abuse. Screening of persons employed in child care is a method of child sexual abuse prevention.

Efforts at primary prevention of physical child abuse and neglect focus on targeting at-risk groups such as adolescent parents, impoverished single-parent families, parents expecting their first child, and parents with limited intelligence (see Chapter Four). Effective prevention programs have employed home visits to provide some basic social support and education concerning normal child development, adequate child cognitive stimulation, and parenting strategies. Prevention of physical abuse may also be accomplished by curbing corporal punishment. Corporal punishment by a parent is often associated with later physical abuse by that same parent. Further, physically disciplined children have an increased risk of being aggressive toward their own children and of perpetuating the intergeneration transmission of abuse. Firearms control is also believed to have potential for preventing child abuse fatalities.

Treatment. Treatment of the child can be accomplished in individual or group psychotherapy that uses structured, direct approaches focusing on integrating feelings related to the abuse or neglect. The idea is to help children organize and express their memories and feelings in a manner that facilitates their viewing abuse or neglect as something bad that happened, rather than as indicating stigmatization or destiny. Therapeutic day-care programs have often been used in the treatment of young victims of physical or sexual child abuse and neglect and have been shown to improve social and cognitive skills that were impaired and to increase self-esteem. Behavioral therapies are important to decrease sexualized behaviors of sexually abused children, and case management enhances interagency collaboration for all types of child maltreatment. Psychopharmacologic interventions have been found to be effective for abused children (see Chapters One, Six, and Seven).

Treatment of adult caregivers can be accomplished by providing abusive or neglectful parents and their partners with combinations of social support, anger control, and parent training in appropriate child management strategies. It is also important to diagnose and treat parental depression and substance abuse and sexual disorders if present. Compliance and motivation can be enhanced by the conditions of probation and of child visitation and child custody orders.

Elder Abuse

Domestic elder abuse, institutional elder abuse, and self-abuse constitute the three basic categories of elder abuse. Domestic elder abuse refers to maltreatment of an older person by someone who has a special relationship with the elder (such as a spouse, a sibling, a child, a friend, or a caregiver). Most states recognize the following five types of domestic elder abuse:

Physical abuse: nonaccidental use of physical force that results in bodily injury, pain, or impairment
Sexual abuse: nonconsensual contact
Emotional or psychological abuse: willful infliction of mental or emotional pain by threat, humiliation, or intimidation or by other verbal or nonverbal abusive conduct
Neglect: willful or nonwillful failure by the caregiver to fulfill the caregiving obligations
Financial or material exploitation: unauthorized use of funds, property, or any resources

Institutional abuse refers to the above-mentioned forms of abuse occurring in nursing homes, foster homes, group homes, and board-and-care facilities. Perpetrators of institutional abuse are usually those who have a legal or contractual obligation to provide elder victims with care and protection (such as paid caregivers and professionals).

Self-neglect or self-abuse refers to the neglectful or abusive conduct of an older person directed at himself or herself that threatens the person's health or safety. Self-abuse or self-neglect usually occurs as the result of physical or mental impairment (or when the person is socially isolated).

Prevalence. Elder physical abuse is estimated to affect between 3.2 and 10 percent of the elderly population in the United States. More than 1.5 million persons are estimated to be the victims of elder abuse each year. Of the approximately 10 percent of Americans over sixty-five years of age who are victims of elder abuse, about 4 percent are victims of moderate to severe abuse.

The physical indicators of elder maltreatment consist of bruises, lacerations, punctures, fractures, burns, malnutrition, dehydration, lack of personal care, lack of needed medication, venereal diseases, pain or itching, and bruises or bleeding of external genitalia, vaginal area, or anal area. The behavioral and emotional indicators of elder maltreatment are fear, depression, confusion, anger, ambivalence, and insomnia. Risk factors for elder maltreatment are sociodemographic (nonwhite race, poverty, and advanced age), physical and cognitive functional impairment, and social (living with someone or having no group participation).

Best Practices. Mental health and other health care professionals can make considerable contributions to assessment, prevention, and intervention in conflicts within elderly person–caregiver dyads. Prevention of elder maltreatment requires knowledge of forensic issues, including competency, guardianship needs, and state reporting laws.

The psychiatric evaluation of elderly people needs to be preceded by a comprehensive physical and neurological examination with emphasis placed on the doses, frequencies, and interactions of all current and recent medication. A review of laboratory tests, X-rays, and other imaging techniques indicated by current physical and neurological findings is indicated. It may be necessary to apply the Mini Mental State examination, the Hachinski Scale to rule out multi-infarct dementia, the Geriatric Depression Scale, the Hamilton Rating Scale for Depression, the Older American Resources and Services questionnaire for functional capacity, or the Cambridge Dementia Examination (CAMDEX—a comprehensive instrument that incorporates the information from the caregiver with assessment of dementia and depression). Furthermore, the evaluation of the elderly patient needs to include family assessment, including the elder's role in the family and the possible multiple roles of the caregiver. Finally, the history may be bolstered by collateral information.

All states and the District of Columbia have adopted elder abuse reporting laws, and in most states there is legislation creating elder abuse programs. Ombudsmen from law enforcement; social services; human service, protection, and advocacy agencies; and state nursing homes may be designated to receive and investigate complaints. Interventions for elder abuse vary by state and may include court orders to restrain abusers from having contact with victims, compensation for victims' legal and medical expenses, and treatment for perpetrators.

Advocacy. As in domestic and intimate partner and child and adolescent physical and sexual abuse, psychiatric emergency room staff training is needed.

When the abused elderly person appear to be mentally incompetent, an assessment of capacity needs to be made to determine the person's ability to participate in decision making. If the person appears to lack capacity, a petition for the appointment of a guardian should be filed with the appropriate court.

Family Violence Intervention Program Examples

Abuse Prevention Project, 1320 Grand Ave., Billings, MT 59102, (406) 259-2007, fax (406) 259-4901.

Bolton Refuge House, P.O. Box 482, Eau Claire, WI 54702, (715) 834-0628.

Center for Traumatic Stress in Children and Adolescents, Allegheny General Hospital, Department of Psychiatry, MCP–Hahnemann School of Medicine, 4 Allegheny Center, Room 859, Pittsburgh, PA 15212, (412) 330-4321.

Child Abuse Prevention Program, 217 E. College St., Jackson, TN 38301, (901) 424-7900, fax (901) 424-4847.

Child Protection Team Prevention Project, 340 Beal Parkway, Pittsburgh, PA 32548, (850) 833-3774, fax (850) 883-3897.

Civitas Center, Department of Psychiatry, Baylor University School of Medicine, One Baylor Plaza, Houston, TX 77030, (713) 770-3750.

Domestic Violence Project, 6308 8th Avenue, Kenosha, WI 3143, (414) 656-8502.

Families and Schools Together, P.O. Box 7948 Station C, Atlanta, GA 30357, (404) 853-2800, fax (404) 853-2889.

The Family Center, Presbyterian Hospital, Columbia University Program for Abused and Neglected Children, 622 W. 168th St., Babies Hospital, 6 North, Room 616, New York, NY 10032, (212) 305-6694.

The Family Crisis Program, Division of Child and Adolescent Psychiatry, North Shore University Hospital, New York University School of Medicine, 400 Community Dr., Manhasset, NY 11030, (516) 562-3005.

Family Support Program, P.O. Box 1456, Fort Worth, TX 76101, (817) 535-6462, fax (817) 535-2215.

Hawaii Healthy Start Program, Kapiolani Medical Center for Women and Children, 1833 Kalakaua Ave., Ste. 1001, Honolulu, HI 96815, (808) 944-9000, fax (808) 944-2751.

Parent Education Program, P.O. Box 1707, Dalton, GA 30722, (706) 272-7919, fax (706) 275-6542.

Parent Empowerment/Educational Project, 423 Bryant Ave., North Minneapolis, MN 55405, (612) 377-0778, fax (612) 377-2163.

Queens District Attorney's Elder Abuse Program, Special Victims Bureau, 80-02 Kew Gardens Road, Kew Gardens, NY 11415, (718) 286-6562.

Saint Louis Crisis Nursery, 6150 Oakland Ave., St. Louis, MO 63139, (314) 768-3201, fax (314) 768-3996.

Existing Organizational Policy Statements and Clinical Guidelines

Child Maltreatment

American Academy of Child and Adolescent Psychiatry, 615 Wisconsin Ave., Washington, DC 20016, (202) 966-7000. *Guidelines for the Clinical Evaluation of Child and Adolescent Sexual Abuse.*

American Academy of Pediatrics, Committee on Child Abuse and Neglect. "Guidelines for the Evaluation of Sexual Abuse of Children." *Pediatrics,* 1991, 87, 254–260.

American Medical Association, 535 N. Dearborn St., Chicago, IL, 60610, (312) 464-5066. *Diagnostic and Treatment Guidelines on Child Sexual Abuse.*

American Professional Society on the Abuse of Children, 332 South Michigan Ave., Ste. 1600, Chicago, IL 60604, (312) 554-0166. *Guidelines for Psychosocial Evaluation of Suspected Sexual Abuse in Young Children* (1990); *Descriptive Terminology in Child Sexual Abuse Medical Evaluations* (1995).

American Psychiatric Association, APA Library, 1400 K Street NW, Washington, DC 20005. *Position Statement on Child Abuse and Neglect by Adults.*

Elder Abuse

American Medical Association, Council on Scientific Affairs. "Elder Abuse and Neglect." *Journal of the American Medical Association,* 1987, *25,* 7.

American Medical Association, 535 N. Dearborn St., Chicago, IL 60610, (312) 464-5066. *Diagnostic and Treatment Guidelines on Elder Abuse and Neglect.* (Includes a listing of protective service programs in various states.) Chicago: American Medical Association, 1992.

American Psychiatric Association, APA Library, 1400 K Street, NW, Washington, DC 20005. *Position Statement on Elder Abuse, Neglect and Exploitation* (1994).

Bloom, J., Ansell, P., and Bloom, M. "Detecting Elder Abuse: A Guide for Physicians." *Geriatrics,* 1989, *44,* 40–44.

Carr, K., and others. "Practice Concepts: An Elder Abuse Assessment Team in an Acute Hospital Setting." *Gerontologist,* 1986, *26,* 19.

Tomita, S. "Detection and Treatment of Elderly Abuse and Neglect: A Protocol for Health Care Professionals." *Geriatrics,* 1982, *2* (2), 37–51.

Domestic and Intimate Partner Abuse

American College of Obstetrics and Gynecology, 409 12th St. NW, Washington, DC 20024, (202) 638-5577. *Women's Health: The Abused Woman* (1993).

American Medical Association. *Diagnostic and Treatment Guidelines on Domestic Violence.* American Medical Association: Chicago, 1992.

American Psychiatric Association. "American Psychiatric Association Policy Statement: Domestic Violence Against Women." *American Journal of Psychiatry,* 1994, *151,* 630.

Association of Trial Lawyers of America, 1050 31st St. NW, Washington, DC 20007. *Preventing Violence to Women: Integrating the Health and Legal Communities* (1993).

New York State Department of Social Services, (518) 473-3170. *Handbook for Abused Women.*

Victim Advocacy and Referral Resources

American Humane Association Children's Division, 9725 E. Hampden Ave., Denver, CO 80231, (800) 227-5242.

Center for Women Policy Studies, 2000 P St. NW, Ste. 508, Washington, DC 20036, (202) 872-1770.

Child Abuse and Neglect Prevention Information Line, (800) 342-7472.

The Family Violence Prevention Fund's Health Resource Center on Domestic Violence, (800) 313-1310.

Marital Rape Information, University of Illinois at Urbana-Champaign, 415 Library, 1408 West Gregory Drive, Urbana, IL 618011, (217) 244-1024.

Missing Children Hotline, (800) 346-3543.

National Aging Resource Center on Elder Abuse, 810 First St. NE, Ste. 500, Washington, DC 20002, (202) 682-2470.

National Center for Missing and Exploited Children, 201 Wilson Blvd., Ste. 500, Arlington, VA 22210, (800) 843-5678.

National Coalition Against Domestic Violence, 1151 K St. NW, Room 409, Washington, DC 20037, (202) 638-6388.
National Coalition Against Sexual Assault, Volunteers of America, 8787 State St., Ste. 202, East St. Louis, IL 12203, (618) 271-9833.
National Committee for the Prevention of Elder Abuse, c/o Institute on Aging, Medical Center of Central Massachusetts, 119 Belmont St., Worcester, MA 01605.
National Council on Child Abuse and Family Violence, 1155 Connecticut Ave. NW, Ste. 400, Washington, DC 20036, (202) 429-6695.
National Crime Prevention Council, 1700 K St. NW, 2nd Floor, Washington, DC 20006, (202) 466-6272.
National Institute on Aging, National Institutes of Health, Public Health Service, U.S. Department of Health and Human Services, Gateway Building, Ste. 533, Bethesda, MD 20892, (301) 496-3136. *Older People in Society.*
National Organization for Victim Assistance, 1757 Park Rd. NW, Washington, DC 20010, (202) 232-6682.
National Resource Center on Domestic Violence, 6400 Flank Dr., Ste. 1300, Harrisburg, PA 15112, (800) 537-2238.
National Resource Center for Foster and Residential Care, Child Welfare Institute, P.O. Box 77364 Station C, Atlanta, GA 30357, (404) 876-1934
National Victims Resource Center, Office for Victims of Crime, Office of Justice Programs, U.S. Department of Justice, Washington, DC 20531, (800) 627-6872, (202) 307-5933.
National Youth Crisis Hotline/Home Runaway Hotline, (800) 448-4663.
Telecommunications Device for the Deaf, National Domestic Violence Hotline, (800) 787-3224.

Additional Resources

Babcock, J.C.D., Waltz, J., Jacobson, N. S., and Gottman, J. M. "Power and Violence: The Relation Between Communication Patterns, Power Discrepancies, and Domestic Violence," Special section: "Couples and Couple Therapy." *Journal of Consulting Clinical Psychology,* 1993, *61,* 40–50.
Beardslee, W. R., and others. "Sustained Change in Parents Receiving Preventive Interventions for Families with Depression." *American Journal of Psychiatry,* 1997, *154,* 510–515.
Cascardi, M., and O'Leary, K. D. "Depressive Symptomatology, Self-Esteem, and Self-Blame in Battered Women." *Journal of Family Violence,* 1992, *7,* 249–259.
Cochran, C., and Petrone, S. "Elder Abuse: The Physician's Role in Identification and Prevention." *Illinois Medical Journal,* 1987, *171,* 241–246.
Commonwealth Fund. *First Comprehensive National Health Survey of American Women.* New York: Commonwealth Fund, 1993.
Davis, L., and Carlson, B. "Observation of Spouse Abuse: What Happens to the Children?" *Journal of Interpersonal Violence,* 1987, *2,* 278–291.
Dodge, K. A., Bates, J. E., and Pettit, G. S. "Mechanisms in the Cycle of Violence." *Science,* 1990, *250,* 1678–1683.
Egami, Y., Ford, D. E., Greenfield, S. F., and Crum, R. M. "Psychiatric Profile and Sociodemographic Characteristics of Adults Who Report Physically Abusing or Neglecting Children." *American Journal of Psychiatry,* 1996, *153,* 921–928.
Else, D., and others. "Personality Characteristics of Men Who Physically Abuse Women." *Hospital Community Psychiatry,* 1993, *44,* 54–58.
Finkelhor, D., and Pillemer, K. "Elder Abuse: The Relationship to Other Forms of Family Violence." In G. Hotaling, D. Finkelhor, R. Gelles, and M. Straus (eds.), *New Directions in Family Violence.* Thousand Oaks, Calif.: Sage, 1984.
Finkelhor, D., and Yllo, K. "Rape in Marriage: A Sociological View." In D. Finkelhor, R. Gelles, G. Hotaling, and M. Straus (eds.), *In the Dark Side of Families.* Thousand Oaks, Calif.: Sage, 1983.

Fisher, L. J., and others. "Psychosocial Characteristics of Physically Abused Children and Adolescents." *Journal of the American Academy of Child & Adolescent Psychiatry,* 1997, *36,* 123–131.

Gelles, R. J., and Straus, M. A. *Intimate Violence: The Definitive Study of the Causes and Consequences of Abuse in the American Family.* New York: Simon & Schuster, 1988.

Goldstein, M., and Woods C. "Elder Abuse, Neglect, and Exploitation." *American Association for Geriatric Psychiatry Newsletter,* 1993, *13,* 8–9.

Hart, J., Gunnar, M., and Cicchetti, D. "Altered Neuroendocrine Activity in Maltreated Children Related to Symptoms of Depression." *Developmental Psychopathology,* 1996, *8,* 201–214.

Hershorn, M., and Rosenbaum, A. "Children of Marital Violence: A Closer Look at the Unintended Victims." *American Journal of Orthopsychiatry,* 1985, *55,* 260–266.

Hudson, M. J., and Johnson, T. F. "Elder Neglect and Abuse: A Review of the Literature." *Annual Review of Gerontology and Geriatrics,* 1986, *6,* 81–134.

Ito, Y., Teacher, M. H., Clod, C. A., and Ackerman, E. "Preliminary Evidence for Aberrant Cortical Development in Abused Children: A Quantitative EEG study." *Journal of Neuropsychiatry and Clinical Neuroses,* 1998, *10,* 298–307.

Jaffe, P., Wolfe, D., and Wilson, S. *Children of Battered Women.* Thousand Oaks, Calif.: Sage, 1990.

Jensen, J. B., Pease, J. J., Ten Bensel, R., and Garfinkel, E. D. "Growth Hormone Response Patterns in Sexually or Physically Abused Boys." *Journal of American Academy of Child & Adolescent Psychiatry,* 1991, *30,* 784–790.

Kaplan, S. J. (ed.). *Family Violence: A Clinical and Legal Guide.* Washington, D.C.: American Psychiatric Press, 1996.

Kaplan, S. J., and others. "Adolescent Physical Abuse: Risk for Adolescent Psychiatric Disorders." *American Journal of Psychiatry,* 1988, *155,* 954–959.

Kaplan, S. J., and others. "Adolescent Physical Abuse and Suicide Attempts." *Journal of American Academy of Child & Adolescent Psychiatry,* 1997, *36,* 799–808.

Lachs, S., and others. "Risk Factors for Reported Elder Abuse and Neglect: A Nine-Year Observational Cohort Study." *Gerontologist,* 1997, *137,* 469–474.

Luntz, B. K., and Widom, C. S. "Antisocial Personality Disorder in Abused and Neglected Children Grown Up." *American Journal of Psychiatry,* 1994, *151,* 670–674.

Lyons-Ruth, K., Cornell, D. B., Grunebaum, H.U.I., and Botein, S. "Infants at Social Risk: Maternal Depression and Family Support Services as Mediators of Infant Development and Security of Attachment." *Child Development,* 1990, *6,* 85–98.

Malinosky-Rummell, R., and Hansen, D. J. "Long-Term Consequences of Childhood Physical Abuse." *Psychological Bulletin,* 1993, *114,* 68–79.

Mercy, J. A., and Saltzman, L. E. "Fatal Violence Among Spouses in the United States, 1976–85." *American Journal of Public Health,* 1989, *79,* 595–599.

National Center on Elder Abuse and Neglect. *Understanding the Nature of Elder Abuse in Domestic Settings.* Washington, D.C.: National Center on Elder Abuse and Neglect, 1995.

National Research Council Panel on Research on Child Abuse and Neglect, Commission on Behavioral and Social Sciences and Education. *Understanding Child Abuse and Neglect.* Washington, D.C.: National Academy Press, 1993.

Salzinger, S., Feldman, R. S., Hammer, M., and Rosario, M. "The Effects of Physical Abuse on Children's Social Relationships." *Child Development,* 1993, *64,* 169–187.

Sedlak, A., and Broadhurst, D. D. *The Third National Incidence Study of Child Abuse and Neglect.* Washington, D.C.: U.S. Department of Health and Human Services, 1996.

Steimmetz, S. K. "Elder Abuse by Family Caregivers: Processes and Intervention Strategies." *International Journal of Contemporary Family Therapy,* 1988, *10,* 256–271.

Straus, M. A., and Gelles, R. J. *Physical Violence in American Families: Risk Factors and Adaptations to Violence in 8,145 Families.* New Brunswick, N.J.: Transaction, 1990.

Straus, M. A., and Kantor, U. K. "Corporal Punishment of Adolescents by Parents: A Risk Factor in the Epidemiology of Depression, Suicide, Alcohol Abuse, Child Abuse, and Wife Beating." *Adolescence,* 1994, *29,* 543–561.

Straus, M. A., Sugarman, D. B., and Giles-Sims, J. "Spanking by Parents and Subsequent Antisocial Behavior of Children." *Archives of Pediatric Adolescent Medicine,* 1997, *151,* 761–767.

Terr, L. C. "Childhood Traumas: An Outline and Overview." *American Journal of Psychiatry,* 1991, *48,* 10–20.

U.S. Department of Health and Human Services. *Child Maltreatment 1997: Reports from the States to the National Child Abuse and Neglect Data System.* Washington, D.C.: U.S. GPO, 1999.

U.S. House. *Elder Abuse Prevention, Identification, and Treatment Act of 1985.* H.R. 1674, 1985.

Walker, L. "Psychological Causes of Family Violence." In M. Lystad (ed.), *Violence in the Home: Interdisciplinary Perspectives.* New York: Brunner/Mazel, 1986.

Wolf, R. S. "Elder Abuse: Ten Years Later." *Journal of the American Geriatric Society,* 1988, *36,* 758–762.

Wolfe, D., and others. "Children of Battered Women: The Relation of Child Behavior to Family Violence and Maternal Stress." *Journal of Consulting Clinical Psychology,* 1985, *53,* 657–665.

Wolfe, D., Reppucci, N. D., and Hart, S. "Child Abuse Prevention: Knowledge and Priorities." *Journal of Clinical Child Psychology,* 1995, *24,* 1–83 (supplement).

Wolfe, D. A., and Wekerte, C. "Treatment Strategies for Child Physical Abuse and Neglect: A Critical Progress Report." *Clinical Psychology Review,* 1993, *13,* 473–500.

Zuravin, S. J. "Severity of Maternal Depression and Three Types of Mother-to-Child Aggression." *American Journal of Orthopsychiatry,* 1980, *59,* 377–389.

SANDRA J. KAPLAN is professor of clinical psychiatry, New York University School of Medicine, and vice chairman, Department of Psychiatry for Child and Adolescent Psychiatry, North Shore University Hospital, North Shore-Long Island Jewish Health System, Manhasset, New York.

6

Molestation and rape in childhood or adulthood is sexual violence. This chapter discusses issues for sexual violence victims and suggests several best practices for this population.

Sexual Violence: The Victim

Sandra L. Bloom

Victims of sexual violence may experience their first sexual assault as either children or adults.

Childhood Sexual Violence

Childhood sexual violence is usually referred to as sexual abuse and is most commonly associated with someone who is known to the child, usually in the role of caretaker. In five studies of sexual abuse between 1940 and 1978, one-fifth to one-third of all women reported having been sexually abused in childhood (Herman, 1992). A poll of parents estimated nineteen per one thousand suffered sexual abuse (Gallup Organization, 1995). The Third National Incidence Study of Child Abuse found girls are sexually abused three times as often as boys, and though the risk of being sexually abused does not vary among races, children from lower income groups or from single-parent families are more frequently victims (U.S. Department of Health and Human Services, 1996). Furthermore, from age three on, children are at a constant rate of risk, meaning an especially broad range of vulnerability throughout their childhood (Sedlak and Broadhurst, 1996). Finally, the number of sexually abused children in the United States rose by 83 percent from 1986 to 1993 (U.S. Department of Health and Human Services, 1996). In the United States, more than six out of ten of all rape cases (61 percent) involved victims under eighteen, and 29 percent of all forcible rape involves victims under the age of eleven (National Victim Center, 1993). Of the adolescents ages twelve to seventeen in the United States, an estimated 8 percent have been victims of serious sexual assault (Kilpatrick and Saunders, 1997).

Sexual abuse in childhood often results in prolonged exposure to overwhelming stress and conflict. A large study of female adults sexually abused

New Directions for Mental Health Services, no. 86, Summer 2000 © Jossey-Bass as children found that the abuse lasted an average of 7.6 years and began at age six. Fifty-three percent were abused by biological fathers, nearly 15 percent by stepfathers, and 8.8 percent by uncles. Only 6.2 percent of the perpetrators were female. The study also found that the younger the child is when he or she reveals the abuse, the more negative and unsupportive the reaction he or she receives. In 77.2 percent of the cases in which the disclosure was made during childhood, the abuse continued for at least one year (Roesler, 1994). Recent research suggests that at an initial intervention, child sex abuse victims are equally traumatized regardless of whether the perpetrators were intra- or extrafamilial (Whitcomb, 1994).

The long-term consequences of sexual assault in childhood are extensive. Child sexual abuse has been found to be comorbid with many later psychiatric and physical problems (see Chapter Seven). In a review of long-term consequences, Polusny and Follette (1995) found that sexually abused subjects report higher levels of general psychological distress and higher rates of both major psychological disorders and personality disorders than nonabused subjects do. Adult survivors of child sexual abuse report poorer social and interpersonal functioning; greater sexual dissatisfaction, dysfunction, and maladjustment including high-risk sexual behavior; and a greater tendency toward revictimization through adult sexual assault and physical partner violence. In a study of men sexually abused as children, more than 80 percent had a history of substance abuse; 50 percent had suicidal thoughts; 23 percent had attempted suicide; and almost 70 percent had received psychological treatment. Thirty-one percent had violently victimized others (Lisak, 1994). Among children who were sexually abused, the odds are 27.7 times higher than the odds for nonvictims that they will be arrested for prostitution as adults (Widom and Ames, 1995). Comparing long-term gender differences, there seems to be a greater likelihood that men who were sexually abused as children will express some sexual interest in children (Finkelhor, 1994).

Adult Sexual Assault

Estimates for adult sexual assault also support the proposition that most violence directed against women is perpetrated by intimates. Twenty-two percent of women polled say they have been forced to do sexual things against their will, usually by an intimate (Laumann, 1994). In 1990, 683,000 American women were forcibly raped, which equals 56,916 per month, 1,871 per day, 78 per hour, and 1.3 per minute; only 16 percent were reported to the police (Kilpatrick and Edmunds, 1992). One out of every eight adult women, or at least 12.1 million American women, will be the victim of forcible rape at some point in her lifetime (Kilpatrick and Edmunds, 1992). In 1994, the rape and sexual assault rate for females was 3.7 per 1,000 persons aged twelve or older—a total of 407,190 victimizations. The rape and sexual assault rate for males was 2 per 1,000 persons aged twelve or older, a total of 25,570 victimizations (Bureau of Justice Statistics, 1997). Another survey revealed that 1,000 rapes were reported on college campuses during 1991–92 academic year (Nichols, 1995).

The effects of victimization often generate psychiatric dysfunction and are of special interest to mental health professionals. In a survey of victimization experiences in more than two thousand women, rates of "nervous breakdowns," suicidal ideation, and suicide attempts were significantly higher for crime victims than for nonvictims. Nearly one rape victim in five (19.2 percent) had attempted suicide, whereas only 2.2 percent of nonvictims had done so. Most sexual assault victims' mental health problems appeared after their victimization (Kilpatrick and others, 1985).

The prevalence of posttraumatic stress disorder (PTSD) after rape is extraordinarily high. De Girolamo and McFarlane (1996) have reviewed nine studies that investigated the prevalence of PTSD among victims of rape or other sexual violence. In four studies the rate was greater than 70 percent and less than 25 percent in only five studies. Kessler and others (1995) found similar rates in men (46.4 percent) and women (48.4 percent). In addition, the prevalence of other psychiatric comorbidity after sexual victimization is higher than in the general population.

Women who are victimized also have a greater rate of physical comorbidity. Rape and life-threatening physical abuse seem to have worse health effects than do less serious physical violence and milder forms of sexual abuse. One study of 239 female patients with gastrointestinal disorders found that 66.5 percent of the women had experienced sexual or physical abuse. Furthermore, women with sexual abuse history had more pain, other somatic symptoms, bed disability days, lifetime surgeries, and functional disabilities than those without sexual abuse (Leserman and others, 1996). Walker and others (1996) looked at the comorbidity between chronic pelvic pain, irritable bowel syndrome, and a history of abuse. They found that compared with women with irritable bowel syndrome alone, those with both irritable bowel syndrome and chronic pelvic pain were significantly more likely to have a lifetime history of dysthymic disorder, current and lifetime panic disorder, somatization disorder, childhood sexual abuse, and hysterectomy. In a randomized survey of 1,599 women, 31.5 percent of participants reported a diagnosis of gynecological problems in the past five years. Those with problems were more likely to report childhood abuse, violent crime victimization, and spouse abuse (Plichta and Abraham, 1996). Another study looked at the connection between chronic intractable pain and histories of childhood sexual abuse in 112 women sampled from a large university campus health center. Fifty-nine women with chronic back pain were sampled and compared with fifty-three control subjects obtained simultaneously from the same clinical population. The women with chronic intractable back pain had a significantly higher percentage of childhood sexual abuse experiences than the controls did (Pecukonis, 1996).

Costs of Sexual Violence

In 1991, one in five, or about 61,000, offenders in state prisons had been convicted of a crime against a victim who was under eighteen years of age (Greenfeld, 1996). Although an estimated 22 percent of child victimizers reported having been sexually abused, less than 6 percent of adult victimizers reported such backgrounds. Among all violent offenders with a history of having been sexually abused, nearly half had child victims. Among all violent offenders with a history of having been physically abused, nearly 30 percent had child victims. Among violent offenders with no history of physical or sexual abuse, 15.5 percent had child victims. About 95 percent of child victimizers and 86 percent of adult victimizers who reported having been abused physically or sexually said that such abuse had occurred while they were children. Among those who suffered physical or sexual abuse before age eighteen, 36 percent had child victims; among those who suffered abuse after entering adulthood, 13 percent had child victims. For about nine out of ten violent offenders experiencing prior physical or sexual abuse, the abuser was someone they had known. For both inmates with child victims and inmates with adult victims, about half reported that the abuse they suffered was perpetrated by a parent or guardian (Greenfeld, 1996).

In a study of serial rapists serving time in U.S. prisons, 56.1 percent were judged to have at least one forced or exploitative abuse experience in boyhood, as compared with the group in a study of 2,972 college males, 7.3 percent of whom reported experiencing boyhood sexual abuse. Also, the rapist sample revealed higher rates of a family member as abuser than the college sample. When the researchers obtained more details from the rapists on their sexual activities as boys, they found that 51 percent reenacted their own abuse as preadolescents, their earliest victims being girls they knew in the neighborhood, their sisters, or girlfriends. Rape fantasies in midadolescence emerged as spying, fetish burglaries, molestations, and rapes. Finally, these juvenile behaviors established a pattern of criminal behavior as these men sought out their next group of victims—strangers (Burgess, 1988).

Rivera and Widom (1990) looked at the criminal histories for substantiated cases of physical and sexual abuse and neglect (908 cases) in one Midwestern county from the years 1967 through 1971. They compared these cases with the histories of individuals who had no official record of abuse or neglect. Childhood victimization increased the overall risk for violent offending, particularly for males and African Americans. Luntz and Widom (1994) looked at these cases and discovered that childhood victimization was a significant predictor of the number of lifetime symptoms of antisocial personality disorder and of a diagnosis of antisocial personality disorder. Another group of researchers studied children nine to fourteen years of age who were sexual offenders. The sex offenders were found to exhibit a significant history of nonsexual antisocial behavior, physical abuse, and psychiatric comorbidity: 65 percent of the boys had been sexually abused (Shaw and others, 1993). Browne and Bassuk (1997) studied 436 homeless and poorhoused women and found that 42 percent were victims of childhood sexual molestation and that 83 percent had very low income mothers who had been victims of severe physical or sexual violence.

Another way of looking at costs is to attempt valuations based on specific kinds of traumatic events. For example, every incident of child sexual abuse has been estimated to cost the victim and society at least $99,000 (Miller, Cohen, and Wiersema, 1996).

Normative standards about the acceptability of the sexual assault of women remain confused. In a 1993 national study of 1,700 sixth- to ninth-graders, a majority of the boys considered rape "acceptable" under certain conditions, and many of the girls agreed (Wallis, 1995). According to several sources, 51 to 60 percent of college men report that they would rape a woman if they were certain that they could get away with it. One out of twelve college men surveyed had committed acts that met the legal definition of rape; 84 percent of these men said what they did was definitely not rape (Warshaw, 1988).

Finally, system responses are often considered to be inadequate. Forty-three percent of responding physicians indicated that multidisciplinary centers responding to child sex abuse were occasionally, rarely, or never adequate (Kerns, Terman, and Larson, 1994). Unfortunately, many of our most resistant social problems have a relationship to a history of sexual violence.

Best Practices

Unfortunately, because well done research on how to treat victims of sexual violence is limited, clinical experience must inform best practices for this population.

Training. Clinicians need to be thoroughly trained in recognizing the signs and symptoms of PTSD, dissociative disorders, other complex trauma-related syndromes, and the many masked and comorbid presentations associated with a history of sexual violence. One of the obstacles to recognizing the markers of sexual violence is the continuing social (including psychiatric) denial of the frequency with which children are sexually abused. Unresolved childhood experiences on the part of the clinician can also be an obstacle to recognizing sexual abuse in patients. Accordingly, clinicians should be trained to routinely screen for a history of sexual violence in childhood and in adulthood.

Safety. Assessing the individual's present level of safety is critical to good management.

Clinicians who work with children and adolescents must be thoroughly versed in their state's reporting laws as well as in the services that are available in the community for victims and their families. Treatment cannot be effective as long as safety issues remain paramount in the treatment setting (see Chapter Seven).

Self-Destructive Behavior. Addressing safety concerns must include a thorough evaluation and the development of a treatment plan to address all self-destructive behavior (suicidality, self-mutilation, or substance abuse disorders) as well as violent behavior directed at others. Unsafe practices such as dangerous, excessive, or addictive sexual practices; other forms of risk-taking behaviors; involvement in dangerous relationships; and excessive working or exercising must also be assessed. Violence directed at others may be the primary manifestation of the patient's clinical presentation or may be very carefully disguised. Victims often experience extreme shame about their inability to control their own impulses toward perpetration, particularly against children. Clinicians must become comfortable in asking frank questions about violent impulses, wishes, fantasies, and actions (see Chapter Seven).

Goal Setting. Treatment of traumatized victims, particularly those suffering from the complex syndromes associated with childhood sexual abuse, may require years. As a result, treatment contracts, focused goal setting, and optimally, a team treatment approach are critical. The goals of treatment should focus on

The development of authority over the remembering process so that the past stops haunting the present
The integration of memory and affect
The ability to tolerate affect
The mastery of symptoms
The development of self-esteem and self-cohesion
The ability to create and sustain safe attachment relationships
The need to make sense out of one's previous negative life experiences, place them in some form of life narrative, and ultimately transform those experiences into a survivor mission (Harvey, 1996)

Although it is often necessary for a victim to review previous experiences in detail, it is important that the ability to function in the present is supported and promoted.

Memory. Clinicians need to keep current about the latest advances in memory science—both in the ways memory can be influenced and altered as well as in the ways traumatic memory appears to differ from normal memory. Competent clinicians recognize that memory is fallible and that certain therapeutic approaches may increase the likelihood of distortion or confabulation. Hypnosis or amytal interviews that are conducted for the purpose of uncovering past experiences and that contain suggestions regarding possible trauma may also produce false memories. Thus neither procedure should contain suggestions that affect post-hypnotic or post-amytal memories. Clinicians should be aware that in some states, when a client is hypnotized or given amytal, he or she may not be allowed to testify thereafter in any kind of civil or criminal legal proceeding. For childhood sexual abuse, psychiatrists, as health care providers, have a duty to report sexual abuse. In cases of adult recall of childhood sexual violence, it is the responsibility of the patient to seek confirmation of any previous memories. Unless there are current issues of physical safety at stake, clinicians should urge patients to address the work of trauma resolution and symptom reduction before making any major life changes, including confronting alleged perpetrators or engaging in legal action regarding the abuse.

Psychoeducation. Patient education is critical to the process of recovery from sexual trauma. Psychoeducation about the effects of traumatic experience on the body, the concept of the self, relationships with others, and one's overall adjustment helps empower patients to make changes that are critical for recovery. This is particularly important in eliciting the necessary commitment to give up self-destructive behavior.

Medication. Medication is frequently necessary to effectively manage many of the comorbid and presenting symptoms of trauma-related disorders. Patients require treatment for depression, overwhelming anxiety, and co-accompanying psychotic symptoms. The clinician must also be aware that the pursuit of a medical cure in this population can easily become a substitute for the painful work of trauma resolution, leading both the patient and the doctor on an endless search for the right drug. Such practices can lead to abuse, addiction, and polypharmacy with all the attendant risks.

Supervision and Consultation. Clinicians who work with trauma victims are at risk for secondary traumatic stress, also called vicarious traumatization and compassion fatigue. This places clinicians at risk for various negative physical, psychological, relational, spiritual, and professional consequences. The professional consequences include a decrease in the quality and quantity of work, low motivation, avoidance of job tasks, increase in mistakes including boundary violations, setting perfectionist standards, obsession about details, decrease in confidence, loss of interest, dissatisfaction, negative attitude, apathy, demoralization, withdrawal from colleagues, impatience, decrease in quality of relationships, poor communication, staff conflicts, absenteeism, exhaustion, faulty judgment, irritability, tardiness, irresponsibility, overwork, and frequent job changes (Yassen, 1995). The best antidote to the undesirable professional consequences of this exposure is regular supervision.

References

Browne, A., and Bassuk, S. S. "Intimate Violence in the Lives of Homeless and Poor-housed Women: Prevalence and Patterns in an Ethnically Diverse Sample." *American Journal of Orthopsychiatry*, 1997, 67(2), 261–278.

Bureau of Justice Statistics. *Crime and Victims Statistics, Crime Facts at a Glance, Victim Characteristics.* U.S. Department of Justice, Washington, D.C.: U.S. GPO, 1997.

Burgess, A. W., and others. "Serial Rapists and Their Victims: Reenactment and Repetition." *Annals of the New York Academy of Science*, 1988, 528, 277–295.

De Girolamo, G., and McFarlane, A. C. "Epidemiology of Posttraumatic Stress Disorder Among Victims of Intentional Violence: A Review of the Literature." In F. L. Mak and C. C. Nadelson (eds.), *International Review of Psychiatry*, Vol. 2. Washington, D.C.: American Psychiatric Press, 1996.

Finkelhor, D. "Current Information on the Scope and Nature of Child Sexual Abuse." *Future Child*, 1994, 4(2), 31–53.

Gallup Organization. *Disciplining Children in America: A Gallup Poll Report*. Princeton, NJ: Gallup Organization, 1995.

Greenfeld, L. A. *Child Victimizers: Violent Offenders and Their Victims*. Bureau of Justice Statistics, U.S. Department of Justice. Washington, D.C.: U.S. GPO, 1996.

Harvey, M. R. "An Ecological View of Psychological Trauma and Trauma Recovery." *Journal of Traumatic Stress*, 1996, 9(1), 3–23.

Herman, J. L. *Trauma and Recovery*. New York: Basic Books, 1992.

Kerns, D. L., Terman, D. L., and Larson, C. S. "The Role of Physicians in Reporting and Evaluating Child Sexual Abuse Cases." *Future Child*, 1994, 4(2), 119–134.

Kessler, R., and others. "Posttraumatic Stress Disorder in the National Comorbidity Survey." *Archives of General Psychiatry*, 1995, 52, 1048–1060.

Kilpatrick, D. G., and others. "Mental Health Correlates of Criminal Victimization: A Random Community Survey." *Journal of Consulting Clinical Psychology*, 1985, 53(6), 866–873.

Kilpatrick, D. G., Edmunds, C. N., and Seymour, A. K. *Rape in America: A Report to the Nation*. Arlington, Va.: National Victim Center, 1992.

Kilpatrick, D. G., and Saunders, B. *The Prevalence and Consequences of Child Victimization: Summary of a Research Study by Dean Kilpatrick, Ph.D., and Benjamin Saunders, Ph.D.* Washington, D.C.: U.S. Department of Justice, National Institute of Justice, 1997.

Laumann, E. *The Social Organization of Sexuality: Sexual Practices in the United States.* Chicago: University of Chicago Press, 1994.

Leserman, J., and others. "Sexual and Physical Abuse History in Gastroenterology Practice: How Types of Abuse Impact Health Status." *Psychosomatic Medicine*, 1996, 58(1), 4–15.

Lisak, D. "The Psychological Impact of Sexual Abuse: Content Analysis of Interviews with Male Survivors." *Journal of Traumatic Stress*, 1994, 7(4), 525–548.

Luntz, B. K., and Widom, C. S. "Antisocial Personality Disorder in Abused and Neglected Children Grown Up." *American Journal of Psychiatry*, 1994, 151, 670–674.

Miller, T. R., Cohen, M., and Wiersema, B. *Victim Costs and Consequences: A New Look*. Washington, D.C.: U.S. Department of Justice, National Institute of Justice, 1996.

National Victim Center. *Crime and Victimization in America: Statistical Overview*. Arlington, Va.: National Victim Center, 1993.

Nichols, W. D. "Violence on Campus: The Intruded Sanctuary." *The FBI Law Enforcement Bulletin*, 1995, 64(6), 1–6.

Pecukonis, E. V. "Childhood Sex Abuse in Women with Chronic Intractable Back Pain." *Social Work and Health Care*, 1996, 23(3), 1-16.

Plichta, S. B., and Abraham, C. "Violence and Gynecologic Health in Women More Than 50 Years Old." *American Journal of Obstetrics and Gynecology*, 1996, 174(3), 903–907.

Polusny, M. A., and Follette, V. M. "Long-Term Correlates of Child Sexual Abuse: Theory and Review of the Empirical Literature." *Applied and Preventive Psychology*, 1995, 4(3), 143–166.

Rivera, B., and Widom, C. "Childhood Victimization and Violent Offending." *Violence and Victims*, 1990, 5, 19–35.

Roesler, T. A. "Reactions to Disclosure of Childhood Sexual Abuse: The Effect on Adult Symptoms." *Journal of Nervous and Mental Diseases*, 1994, 182(11), 618–624.

Sedlak, A., and Broadhurst, D. D. *The Third National Incidence Study of Child Abuse and Neglect*. Washington, D.C.: U.S. Department of Health and Human Services, 1996.

Shaw, J. A., and others. "Young Boys Who Commit Serious Sexual Offenses: Demographics, Psychometrics, and Phenomenology." *Bulletin of the American Academy of Psychiatry and Law*, 1993, 21(4), 399–408.

U.S. Department of Health and Human Services. *The Third National Incidence Study of Child Abuse and Neglect*. Washington, D.C.: GPO, 1996.

Walker, E. A., and others. "Chronic Pelvic Pain and Gynecological Symptoms in Women with Irritable Bowel Syndrome." *Journal of Psychosomatic Obstetrics and Gynecology*, 1996, 17(1), 39–46.

Wallis, S. "Discipline and Civility Must Be Restored to America's Public Schools." *USA Today Magazine*, 1995, 124, 32–35.

Warshaw, D. *I Never Called It Rape*. New York: HarperCollins, 1988.

Whitcomb, D. *The Child Victim as a Witness: Research Report*. Washington, D.C.: U.S. Department of Justice, Office of Juvenile Justice and Delinquency Prevention, 1994.

Widom, C. P., and Ames, M. A. "Criminal Consequences of Childhood Sexual Victimization." *Child Abuse and Neglect*, 1995, 18(4), 303–318.

Yassen, J. "Preventing Secondary Traumatic Stress Disorder." In C. R. Figley (ed.), *Compassion Fatigue: Coping with Secondary Traumatic Stress Disorder in Those Who Treat the Traumatized*. New York: Brunner/Mazel, 1995.

SANDRA L. BLOOM is executive director of the Sanctuary Programs at Horsham Clinic, Ambler, Pennsylvania, and Hampton Hospital, Rancocas, New Jersey, and author of Creating Sanctuary: Toward the Evolution of Sane Societies.

7

*In addition to assessing and treating victims of sexual vio-
lence, mental health professionals are also called upon to
provide similar services for sexually violent perpetrators.
This chapter addresses these concerns along with the forensic issues surrounding those who commit sexual violence.*

Sexual Violence: The Perpetrator

Bradley R. Johnson

There is a large spectrum of diversity among individuals who commit sexual offenses in terms of their age, background, ethnicity, education,
income level, and marital status. Some sexual offenders are passive or
unassertive whereas others are frequently aggressive. Some limit their
deviant activity to their own children or relatives whereas others victim-
ize extrafamilial individuals or both. There is no single profile of a sexual
offender.

Some individuals who commit sexual offenses have a normal pattern
of sexuality but act out impulsively or opportunistically in a sexually
deviant manner when under the influence of drugs or alcohol or during
stressful situations. Other individuals develop a pattern of consistent deviant
sexual interests or behaviors, also known as *paraphilias*. Paraphilias are
demonstrable sexual fantasies or patterns of behavior that involve nonhu-
man objects and the suffering or humiliation of oneself, one's partner, children, or nonconsenting persons for a period of at least six months. The
sexually arousing fantasies and urges are recurrent and intense, and the person who suffers from the paraphilia has either acted on the fantasies or suffered serious distress because of them.

The majority of offenders suffer from more than one paraphilic behavior. For example, an individual who commits child molestation may also
engage in other sexually deviant behaviors such as exhibitionism,
voyeurism, or rape. Many sexual offenders begin their deviant behaviors in
adolescence, although it is not clear to what degree adolescent sexual
offenders continue to commit offenses into adulthood. It is likely easier to
intervene and treat an adolescent who has not become entrenched in
deviant patterns of behavior than it is to treat adults.

73

Assessment

An integrative biopsychosocial approach to assessment and treatment is the best. Theories as to why individuals commit sexual offenses range from biological determinisms to cognitive/behavioral, family, and societal impetuses. The assessment of sexual perpetrators is a specialized field and should be conducted only by individuals who have been adequately trained and appropriately supervised. The evaluation of a sexual offender both focuses on the risks and the needs of the offender and identifies biological, psychiatric, social, and sexual risk factors that may contribute to his or her sexual deviance. Many mental health professionals (MHPs) may need to seek consultation from specialized experts.

Evaluators should be fair, impartial, and objective but keep in mind the limitations of the information they receive, especially in cases of the offender's self-report. Any evaluation conducted without collateral information should be interpreted cautiously. Offender self-reports are not reliable, as they may deny or distort the truth. A thorough review of written documentation and collateral interviews should include gathering and reviewing information from all available and relevant sources including

Criminal investigation records
Child protection service investigations
Previous evaluations and treatment progress reports
Mental health records and assessments
Medical records
Correctional system reports
Probation and parole reports
Offense statements from the abuser
Offense statements from the victim

The evaluation procedures may include a clinical interview, paper-and-pencil testing, intellectual assessment, and physiological assessment. There is no specific test that must be done as part of the assessment for it to be complete or correct. In addition to interviewing the alleged abuser, the offender's significant other or family of origin or both should be interviewed when possible. Information gathered in the evaluation process includes (but is not limited to) psychiatric history, medical history, family history, history of victimization, education and occupation history, criminal history, history of violence and aggression, interpersonal relationship history, substance abuse, mental status, and a detailed sexual history. The sexual history should include sexual behaviors, sexual development, dating history, intimate sexual contacts, gender identity issues, sexual practices, masturbation practices, sexual dysfunction, fantasy content, and sexually deviant thoughts or behaviors. It should also include questions regarding cognitive distortions about sexuality and an assessment of social competence and impulse control.

Regarding sexually deviant behavior, the evaluator should explore the description of the alleged offense behaviors, the number of victims, the gender and the age of the victims, the frequency and duration of the abusive sexual contact, and the victim selection. Additionally, the offender should be questioned about access to victims; grooming behaviors; the use of threats, coercion, or bribes; the degree of force; and the sexual arousal patterns before, during, and after the offense. The degree of similarity or disparity between the offender and the victim's statements should be noted, as should the alleged offender's explanation for false allegations.

Treatment should be part of the overall recommendations, keeping in mind both community safety and the degree to which an abuser is capable and willing to manage risk. The evaluation focuses on both the risks and needs of the sexual abuser, as well as identifying factors from social and sexual history that may contribute to sexual deviance. Evaluations provide the basis for the development of comprehensive treatment plans and should include recommendations regarding the intensity of intervention, the specific treatment protocol needed, amenability to treatment, and the identified risk the abuser presents to the community.

Psychiatric profiles and clinical assessments do not prove or disprove with complete assurance an individual's propensity to act in a sexually deviant manner or that an individual committed a specific deviant act. Current methods for determining the risk of recidivism of sexual offenders demonstrate at least moderate predictability. Because there is no pure actuarial method yet to assess sexual recidivism, the best prediction is based on the combination of information received from imperfect actuarial assessments mixed with clinical opinion. As further research occurs, it is likely that better actuarial rating tools will be developed, allowing for increasingly better prediction.

Treatment

Sexual deviance is a complicated and multidetermined behavioral disorder. Therefore, treatment should be multimodal in approach, taking into account a biopsychosocial model. The determination as to whether a patient receives treatment as an outpatient versus an inpatient should be based on his or her propensity to re-offend and on the safety of the community.

Treatment for sexual offenders has been found to be most effective when it is multimodal in approach, addressing such issues as admitting guilt, accepting responsibility, identifying deviant cycles, addressing biological precursors, improving social skills, and developing a relapse prevention plan. Deviant sexual arousal may be a crucial part of a cycle of events that lead to sexual offense, and the offender needs to learn how to interrupt this cycle before he or she commits further sexual offenses.

Before engaging in treatment, the sexual perpetrator should receive appropriate information for his or her informed consent regarding reporting laws, confidentiality, and the possible risks and benefits to treatment. Because every sexual offender is different, it is important that treatment interventions are individualized and personalized. Cognitive/behavioral therapy, combined in some cases with psychopharmacological interventions, currently appears to be the most effective method of treatment. Substance abuse treatment, anger control, empathy building, social skills building, and other programs are often used as adjuncts to the basic cognitive/behavioral model.

Pharmacological therapies, including treatment with anti-obsessional agents such as selective serotonin reuptake inhibitors, have been shown to help reduce the impulsive and obsessive nature of some sexual offenders. Other antidepressants and the occasional use of mood stabilizers have been helpful for some. When these medications fail, the use of anti-androgens has shown effectiveness in lowering testosterone levels and libido. Medication treatments, however, should never be used as the sole treatment; they raise ethical concerns in some situations.

Progress in treatment should be based on specific objectives, including observable changes in cognitive processes, arousal patterns, social and sexual functioning and behavioral patterns and the ability to apply newly learned behaviors. Treatment is likely to be much more difficult or may be less effective when the perpetrator denies the offense(s). Treatment has been found to be effective in both group and individual settings, although it is likely a combination of both is most effective. The therapist may find that having permission to work openly with a probation or parole officer is beneficial. Given the high rate of manipulation and deceit in this patient population, frequent use of polygraph and plethysmograph may help in treatment to overcome denial.

Although many sexual offenders have been sexually or physically abused, not all have been abused, nor do all abused individuals become perpetrators. However, a past history of abuse should be addressed in the sex offender's treatment. Victim treatment, however, is not a substitution for perpetrator-specific treatment.

If the deviant sexual behavior is incestuous, the victim should be allowed to have contact with the perpetrator only under certain circumstances. For example, both victim and perpetrator should have received adequate treatment. The victim must feel comfortable in reuniting with the perpetrator. Finally, there should be clearance by the therapists working with both the victim and the perpetrator.

In most cases, treatment is long term. No matter what the setting for initial intensive treatment, most sexual offenders would benefit from continued booster sessions to aid in relapse prevention throughout the majority of their lives. At this time there is no treatment that cures sexual deviancy. Rather, treatment is aimed at reducing or controlling sexual deviant, acting-out behaviors. Sexual offenders who do not receive treatment are felt to be at higher risk for re-offending than those who receive treatment.

MHPs working with sexual offenders should familiarize themselves with practice standards. MHPs working with sexual offenders should examine their own countertransference issues and be comfortable working with this population. They should be familiar with legal and ethical issues related to sexual offense, including state laws concerning reports of child abuse.

Forensic Issues

Recently, a number of states have enacted laws requiring civil commitment and treatment of sexually violent predators with significant or dangerous histories of sexual offense. Although this is an area of controversy to some, we are likely to see an increased number of sexual offenders receiving treatment. Also, with increased prison sentences given to sexual offenders, the necessity for treatment in jails and prisons is increasingly important. Many sexual offenders are receiving lifetime probation, local registration, and community notification as part of their sentences.

Program Examples

Currently, there are a number of programs in the United States and Canada that offer sex offense treatment. These programs vary in their focus and treatment population. Some programs are located in prisons and others in community settings. Some are for adults and others for adolescents. Most treat male offenders. A few focus on female offenders. It is not the intent to describe any specific program in this article. Rather, the reader is referred to the *Sourcebook of Treatment Programs for Sexual Offenders* (Marshall, Fernandez, Hudson, and Ward, 1998) for detailed descriptions. This book is comprehensive and describes programs in all types of settings and throughout the world.

Resources

There are many resources that are available to teach MHPs how to assess and treat sexual perpetrators. The Association for the Treatment of Sexual Abusers thus far has been the leader in this field. The American Academy of Psychiatry and the Law is also an excellent resource. Both organizations have journals that are highly recommended.

Recommendations

Assessment of perpetrators must be biopsychosocial and must include collateral information and a detailed sexual history. Treatment of sexual offenders is most effective when based on a multimodal approach including biological, cognitive, and behavioral therapies. MHPs are strongly encouraged to become educated and more active in the assessment and treatment of sexual offenders, whether in outpatient, inpatient, incarcerated, or civil commitment settings. If not adequately trained in assessing or treating sexual offenders, MHPs should seek appropriate consultation. Basic training in working with sexual offenders should be a part of all MHP educational programs. We need to encourage funding for assessment and treatment from the government and the private sector, including managed care companies. Research that further identifies improved assessment and treatment methods must be encouraged, especially as it regards effective psychopharmacological treatments.

Reference

Marshall, W., Fernandez, Y., Hudson, S., and Ward, T. (eds.). *Sourcebook of Treatment Programs for Sexual Offenders.* New York: Plenum, 1998.

Additional Resources

Barbaree, H., Marshall, W., and Hudson, S. (eds.). *The Juvenile Sex Offender.* New York: Guilford Press, 1993.

Laws, D. R., and O'Donohue, W. (eds.). *Sexual Deviance: Theory, Assessment, and Treatment.* New York, Guilford Press, 1997.

Prentky, R. A., Lee, A.F.S., Knight, R. A., and Cerce, D. A. "Recidivism Rates Among Child Molesters and Rapists: A Methodological Analysis." *Law and Human Behavior,* 1997, *21,* 635–659.

Schwartz, B. K. (ed.). *The Sex Offender.* Vol. 3: *Theoretical Advances, Treating Special Populations, and Legal Developments.* Kingston, N.J.: Civic Research Institute, 1999.

Schwartz, B. K., and H. R. Cellini (eds.). *The Sex Offender.* Vol. 1: *Corrections, Treatment, and Legal Practice.* Kingston, N.J.: Civic Research Institute, 1995.

Schwartz, B. K., and H. R. Cellini (eds.). *The Sex Offender.* Vol. 2: *New Insights, Treatment Innovations, and Legal Developments.* Kingston, N.J.: Civic Research Institute, 1997.

Quinsey, V. L., Rice, M. E., and Harris, G. T. "Actuarial Prediction of Sexual Recidivism." *Journal of Interpersonal Violence,* 1994, *10,* 85–105.

BRADLEY R. JOHNSON *is a private practitioner and assistant professor at the University of Arizona College of Medicine, Department of Psychiatry, and chief of psychiatry for the Arizona Community Protection and Treatment Center, where Arizona's civilly committed sexual offenders receive treatment.*

8

This chapter presents a thorough exposition of treating traumatized patients and victims of violence, addressing many aspects of trauma and victimization critical to a vast proportion of the work that mental health professionals find themselves doing.

Treating Traumatized Patients and Victims of Violence

Richard P. Kluft, Sandra L. Bloom, J. David Kinzie

The impact of traumatic experience on the health, well-being, and development of the individual has been recognized since recorded history. The current understanding of the effects of traumatic experience is a result of the recognition of a delayed posttraumatic response among a significant proportion of returning Vietnam veterans. The simultaneous recognition of the potentially devastating effects of child abuse, rape, domestic violence, disaster, kidnapping, torture, terrorism, and crime victimization led to a recognition that there is a universal human reaction to overwhelming stress. Furthermore, it has been learned that the reaction is biopsychosocial, then mediated through complex individual and social contexts, all of which determine the final outcome of the adaptive process for each individual.

Trauma occurs when both internal and external resources are inadequate to cope with an external threat (van der Kolk, 1989). Trauma means experiencing, witnessing, anticipating, or being confronted with an event or events that involve threatened death, actual serious injury, or threat to the physical integrity of one's self or others (American Psychiatric Association, 1994). The response to the event or events include intense fear, helplessness, or horror. Children may express this response in disorganized or agitated behavior. To a great extent, trauma responses can be understood as normal reactions to abnormal stress. However, some persons exposed to insufficient trauma to satisfy the DSM-IV definition will nonetheless develop a trauma response syndrome, indicating some individual differences in vulnerability. Most agree that it is normal to develop some symptoms associated with posttraumatic conditions transiently (and if severe, these constitute a mental illness: acute stress disorder) and concur that when symptoms persist, this may represent persistent damage

NEW DIRECTIONS FOR MENTAL HEALTH SERVICES, no. 86, Summer 2000 © Jossey-Bass and constitute a mental disorder. Shalev (1996) has hypothesized that post-traumatic stress disorder (PTSD) is best understood as a "biopsychosocial trap" in which there is a permanent alteration of neurobiological processes resulting in hyperarousal and excessive stimulus discrimination, the acquisition of conditioned fear responses to trauma-related stimuli, and altered cognitive schemata and social apprehension. In addition, the forms of trauma have an interpersonal and transgenerational impact and give rise to identifiable and treatable forms of distress and dysfunction in the concerned others and in the offspring of the victim of violence.

Economics of Violence

Every incident of child sexual abuse has been estimated to cost the victim and society at least $99,000. Domestic crime against adults accounts for more than $67 billion a year (Miller, Cohen, and Wiersema, 1996). The National Safe Workplace Institute reports that the average cost to employers of a single episode of workplace violence can amount to $250,000 in lost work time and legal expenses (Anfuso, 1994). Furthermore, 111,000 incidents of workplace violence cost employers an estimated $4.2 billion in 1993 (Yarborough, 1994). Annually, gunshot wounds cost an estimated $126 billion, and knife wounds cost another $51 billion (Miller and Cohen, 1997). When the cost of pain, suffering, and the reduced quality of life is taken into consideration, the cost of crime to victims is an estimated $450 billion a year (Miller, Cohen, and Rossman, 1993).

Epidemiology

Violence is commonplace and claims many victims. Lifetime exposure to traumatic events in the general American population ranges from 60 to 70 percent (Kessler and others, 1995; Norris, 1992; Resnick and others, 1993). It is estimated that 21 percent of Americans have experienced a traumatic stressor in the last year. For example, one out of every eight adult women is raped, and 39 percent of these victims are raped more than once (National Victim Center, 1993). There is an overall lifetime prevalence of 6.5 percent for PTSD, and a thirty-day prevalence of 2.8 percent (van der Kolk, McFarlane, and Weisaeth, 1996).

The kinds of exposure vary. The most common traumatic events, affecting about 15 to 35 percent of the people surveyed, were witnessing someone badly injured or killed; being involved in a fire, flood, or other disaster; and being involved in a life-threatening accident. Also common were life-threatening experiences such as robbery and the sudden tragic death or injury of a close relation (Solomon and Davidson, 1997).

According to the American Medical Association (1992), more than 25 percent of the women in the United States will be abused by a current or former partner some time during their lives. In homes where spousal abuse is occurring, children are abused at a rate that is 1,500 percent higher than the national average (National Victim Center, 1993). The latest National Incidence Study of child abuse indicates that the incidence of maltreatment quadrupled between 1986 and 1993 (U.S. Department of Health and Human Services, 1996). Multiple studies have found that one-fifth to one-third of all women reported having had a childhood sexual encounter with an adult male (Herman, 1992). Jenkins and Bell (1997) report on several studies done between 1982 to 1995 in which 26 to 55 percent of youths surveyed reported they had witnessed a shooting or stabbing. One out of every four employees was harassed, threatened, or attacked at work between July 1992 and July 1993 (Yarborough, 1994). Statistics from the U.S. Department of Justice indicate that 83 percent of Americans will be victims of violent crime at some point in their lives, and about 25 percent will be victims of three or more violent crimes (Walinsky, 1995).

Patients with mental illness may be predisposed both to victimization and revictimization. Both the stigmatization of mental illness and the increased vulnerability due to the deficits associated with severe mental illness render those suffering from mental disorders more likely to be mistreated (Bell, Taylor-Crawford, Jenkins, and Chalmers, 1988; Jenkins, Bell, Taylor, and Walker, 1989).

The Gamut of Trauma Responses

Overall, 20 to 25 percent of those exposed to DSM-IV criterion trauma develop PTSD. Because victimization and traumatization are common human experiences occurring to persons with a wide range of premorbid personality styles, ego strengths, diatheses for mental and physical illnesses, social supports, intercurrent stressors, and cultural backgrounds, there is no universal profile for victims of violence. Millions of traumatized individuals go unrecognized and untreated. Furthermore, many specific populations are highly traumatized, including refugees, who in addition to trauma, also face the social and psychological disruption of losing their homeland (Kinzie and Boehnlein, 1993). Studies demonstrate that between 30 to 50 percent of refugees suffer chronic PTSD symptoms. Yet, although the core symptoms of PTSD occur in all cultures, their expression may vary widely across cultures (Kinzie, forthcoming).

The more one is exposed to trauma, in terms of severity and duration, the more likely one is to develop PTSD. For example, among U.S. soldiers in Vietnam, merely being a soldier was associated with a 17 percent rate of PTSD, experiencing median levels of combat with a 28 percent rate of PTSD, and being exposed to heavy levels of combat with a 65 percent rate of PTSD (van der Kolk, McFarlane, and Weisaeth, 1996). Early or prior experiences of trauma make a trauma victim more vulnerable to developing posttraumatic symptoms and may increase the severity of those symptoms. Thus, when PTSD is complicated by both childhood and later adult trauma, it is one of the most difficult and complex disorders to treat and may have strong characterological components as well.

Although many people appear to recover from trauma without intervention, many do not, and they require ongoing attention to their distress and dysfunction. Some trauma victims experience delayed onset of posttraumatic symptoms, even decades after the exposure to DSM-IV criterion trauma. Posttraumatic symptoms may wax and wane in intensity, and there may be asymptomatic periods. Reactivation or exacerbation of posttraumatic symptoms may be triggered by anniversaries of the traumatic events, other stressors (including trauma falling short of the DSM-IV criterion trauma), and both gross and subtle stimuli reminiscent, suggestive, or symbolic of the criterion trauma.

The short-term sequelae of trauma may include reexperiencing the traumatic event in several ways: avoidance of stimuli associated with the trauma, defensive numbing, dissociative symptoms, symptoms of increased arousal, problems with affective regulation, somatization, demoralization, and psychobiological abnormalities such as extreme autonomic responses to stimuli related to the trauma. Long-term sequelae of trauma may include the persistence of the short-term sequelae, with chronic characterological changes such as chronic guilt and shame, a sense of personal helplessness and ineffectiveness, a sense of being permanently damaged, difficulties trusting or maintaining relationships with others, and vulnerability to revictimization or becoming a perpetrator or both. Autonomic dysregulation, neuroendocrine dysfunction, and neuroanatomic lesions may occur.

The Elements of the Trauma Response

The traumatic event is persistently reexperienced in one or more of the following ways:

Recurrent and intrusive distressing recollections of the event, dreams of the event, acting or feeling as if the event were recurring, distress, or psychophysiological reactivity upon exposure to inner or outer cues that symbolize or resemble aspects of the event(s).

Avoidance of stimuli associated with the trauma and numbing of general responsiveness as manifested by efforts to avoid thoughts, feelings, or conversations associated with the trauma; efforts to avoid activities, places, or people that arouse recollections of the trauma; amnesia for aspects of the trauma; diminished interest or participation in significant activities; detachment or estrangement from others; restricted range of affect; and a foreshortened sense of the future. Meaningful attachments may be lost, and the person may fail to participate in planning or preparing for the future.

Dissociative symptoms, such as numbing, detachment, or an absence of emotional responsiveness; a diminished awareness of one's surroundings (such as "being in a daze" or "trancing out"); problems with concentration and attention; derealization; depersonalization; and dissociative amnesia.

Persistent symptoms of increased arousal, such as difficulty falling or staying asleep, irritability or outbursts of anger; difficulty concentrating; hypervigilance; and an exaggerated startle response.

Problems in regulating affective arousal, such as chronic affect dysregulation; difficulty modulating anger; self-destructive and suicidal behavior; difficulty modulating sexual involvement; and impulsive and risk-taking behaviors.

Somatization, including so-called body memories in which the physical sensations associated with traumatization recur in a manner analogous to a flashback, without conscious connection with the traumatic scenario in which the physical sensations were experienced.

Chronic characterological changes, such as alterations in self-perception, including chronic guilt and shame, self-blame, a sense of personal helplessness or ineffectiveness; a sense of being permanently damaged; alterations in one's perception of the perpetrator, including adopting distorted beliefs or idealizing the perpetrator; and alterations in relationships with others, including an inability to trust or maintain relationships with others, revictimization, and victimizing others.

Alterations in one's systems of meaning, such as loss of trust, hope, and sense of energy (despair); loss of "thought as experimental action"; loss of previously sustaining beliefs; and loss of belief in the future.

Psychobiological abnormalities, including extreme autonomic responses to stimuli reminiscent of the trauma, hyperarousal to intense but neutral stimuli, elevated urinary catecholamines, decreased resting glucocorticoids and glucocorticoid responses to stress, decreased serotonin activity (animal studies), increased endogenous opioid response to stimuli reminiscent of trauma, decreased hippocampal volume, and activation of the amygdala and its connections and sensory areas during flashbacks.

Increased vulnerability to physical illnesses and other mental disorders. Some forms of victimization also predispose victims to revictimization. Those persons traumatized by those to whom they also have affectionate and dependent ties often develop a constellation of severe symptoms, problematic dynamics, failures in self-protection, and cognitive distortions that make them more vulnerable to victimization again.

Psychiatric Comorbidity

There is a considerably high rate of comorbid psychiatric disorders in the victimized population. Patients with PTSD were two to four times more likely than those without PTSD to have virtually any other psychiatric disorder, particularly somatization (Solomon and Davidson, 1997). In the study by Breslau, Davis, Andreski, and Peterson (1991), those with PTSD were more than six times as likely to have some other psychiatric disorder.

Kessler and others (1995) found that those with PTSD are almost eight times as likely to have three or more disorders; 88 percent of men and 79 percent of women with PTSD had a history of at least one other disorder. Kessler's study also showed men with PTSD were six to ten times more likely and women four to five times more likely to have affective disorders than were individuals without PTSD. Similar figures appear with anxiety disorders, with men three to seven times more likely and women two to four times more likely to have another anxiety disorder along with their PTSD. It has also been shown that between 25 percent and 58 percent of those seeking substance abuse treatment also were comorbid for PTSD (Grady, 1997). Prolonged exposure to combat, torture, captivity, death and destruction, and repeated sexual abuse can also bring about long-lasting personality change (Herman, Perry, and van der Kolk, 1989; Perry, Herman, van der Kolk, and Hoke, 1990; Pollack, Otto, Rosenbaum, and Sachs, 1992; Southwick, Yehuda, and Giller, 1993). Furthermore, a number of studies have also found correlations between trauma exposure and panic disorder (Pollack, Otto, Rosenbaum, and Sachs, 1992); suicide attempts (Angst, Degonda, and Ernst, 1992); eating disorders (Connors and Morse, 1993); depression, bulimia, and generalized anxiety (Bushnell, Wells, and Oakley-Browne, 1992); chemical dependency (Ellason, Ross, Sainton, and Mayran, 1996); and increased risk for lifetime diagnoses of major depression, panic disorder, phobia, somatization disorder, chronic pain, and drug abuse (Leserman, Toomey, and Drossman, 1995; Walker and others, 1992). The high rate of comorbidity presents particular challenges in assessment of victims. Comorbid disorders, such as depression, may be the victim's primary reason for seeking treatment. Thus, in the face of such high rates of comorbidity, the history of trauma can often be overlooked.

Physical Comorbidity

The evaluation and treatment of victims of violence also requires a team of medical and psychiatric caregivers. Victims present significant difficulties for medical providers who often misdiagnose their medical problems as psychiatric, thus compounding the psychiatric and medical problems. Alternately, they may overdiagnose medical problems that have a psychiatric origin, thus exposing the patient to unnecessary medical and surgical procedures and an increased risk of prescription drug abuse. Many victims also experience physical problems that may be related to the effects of chronic stress on various organ systems or the somatic equivalent of the intrusive sensory phenomena so often associated with PTSD. Sexual and physical abuse results in a greater number of hospital admissions and surgical procedures, somatization, and hypochondriasis in adulthood (Salmon and Calderbank, 1996). Victimization, particularly exposure to chronic trauma, has been associated with many kinds of chronic gastrointestinal symptoms (Drossman, 1995; Fukudo, Nomura, Muranaka, and Taguchi, 1993; Irwin and others, 1996; Leserman and others, 1996; Walker and others, 1992, 1996; also see Chapter Six), chronic pelvic pain (Badura, Reiter, Altmaier, and Rhomberg, 1997; Drossman, 1995; Plichta and Abraham, 1996; Walling and others, 1994; Walker and others, 1996; also see Chapter Six), chronic pain syndromes (Benedikt and Kolb, 1986; Geisser, Roth, Bachman, and Eckert, 1996; Pecukonis, 1996; Walling and others, 1994; also see Chapter Six), fibromyalgia (Amir and others, 1997), asthma, and peptic ulcer (Davidson, Hughes, Blazer, and George, 1991). Koss, Koss, and Woodruff (1991) found that compared with nonvictims, victimized women reported more distress and less well-being, visited the doctor twice as frequently, and had outpatient costs that were 2.5 times greater.

Initial Evaluation

Recognizing victims of violence requires alertness on the part of the examiner to the elements of the trauma response and the symptoms of disorders associated with victimization, a keen appreciation of the fact that many forces may cause a person to withhold a victimization history, and taking enough time to build rapport and perform a comprehensive assessment. Some victims' distress is evident to the observer, whereas other victims contain their pain. Victims of violence should receive an initial evaluation that evaluates all aspects of posttraumatic symptomatology, all posttraumatic sequelae, and all comorbidity thought to be relevant. It is important not to rely on the presence of intrusive symptoms but to give attention to those symptoms associated with avoidance. Imaging techniques to assess for possible changes in brain neuroanatomy, neuroendocrine dysregulation, and neuropsychological assessment of cognitive functioning may be necessary. Specialized interviews to assess the degree of dissociative psychopathology, which commonly accompanies the victimization response and is frequently overlooked, may be indicated. Often treatment founders because the full spectrum of posttraumatic sequelae has not been identified and addressed.

On occasion the patient may be able to recount an accurate history of past victimization at the initial interview. However, the clinician cannot be guaranteed that such information will be forthcoming, for several reasons: shame, memory difficulties, ongoing revictimization or fear of danger, insufficient rapport, or failure to make the connection between life experiences and current symptoms. A thorough evaluation may require several visits, the review of records, interviews with ancillary sources, and additional consultations (such as neurological assessment, psychological testing, and family interviews). Given these potential barriers, the clinician must retain a high index of suspicion, even in the absence of historical details, if the stigmata of victimization are present. At the same time, it is vital that the patients' boundaries be respected and that patients be given the opportunity to explore and reveal their own histories at the pace that is safe for them to do so.

If patients' safety cannot be assured, because they cannot control their impulses toward self-harm, they cannot self-protect, or they are living in circumstances that are life threatening, then the first step in treatment is to achieve safety while properly evaluating the situation. The question of safety is a broad one, encompassing physical, psychological, social, and even moral safety (Bloom, 1997). The initial evaluation must focus on the establishment of a safety contract that may include family and friends as well as the patient. Obvious suicidal ideation or suicide attempts must be taken seriously, regardless of their past frequency. A more subtle differentiation may have to be made in the case of other self-destructive behaviors such as self-mutilation, bingeing and purging, compulsive sexual behaviors, or compulsive risk-taking behaviors that are attempts to manage overwhelming affect. More important than whether or not patients self-mutilate may be whether there has been a change in the patterns of self-mutilation, which may signal a loss of affect control and impulse control that is potentially life threatening. The level of safety will determine the level of care: inpatient, intensive outpatient, partial hospitalization, or outpatient. Victims are often reluctant to seek treatment; therefore the situation is often critical by the time they get to a caregiver. As a result, it is not unusual to find that survivors of victimization, particularly if chronic, require an inpatient hospitalization to stabilize their mental and physical condition, achieve a sense of safety, and begin the process of reeducation and integration. The clinician, however, must be able to assure the patient that the hospital stay will not duplicate previous victimization experiences of captivity, powerlessness, and forced dependency. This mandates that the clinician have available hospital-based resources that can adequately respond to the needs of victims without causing "sanctuary trauma" (Bloom, 1997; Silver, 1986).

Much of the outcome of the evaluation may hinge on how educated the patient is about his or her disorder. Educating the patient from the beginning of treatment about the effects of trauma is a powerful intervention. Because the experience of helplessness is key in understanding the trauma response, efforts should be made from the very first contact to encourage self-empowerment, self-efficacy, and self-control. Patients who have become familiar with the course of their own treatment and who are playing an active role in their care can often provide a clinician unfamiliar with their history with valuable information about their present level of safety.

Many diagnostic errors occur when the clinician, unfamiliar with flashbacks, severe dissociative states, complicated bereavement, and the other intrusive symptoms of trauma, mistakes these symptoms for those of psychosis. Obtaining information from friends and family members or previous caregivers can be an asset in these cases. Patients who have been victimized may appear to be paranoid and unreasonable when the historical details of their experience are lacking, particularly if the attitude of the interviewer triggers their underlying distrust and fears of revictimization. Responding to a terrified trauma victim as if he or she were a dangerous and irrational psychotic can retraumatize the patient and create secondary problems. Inappropriate medication with antipsychotic drugs can produce iatrogenically induced resistance to further treatment. At the same time, however, psychosis and trauma-related syndromes may coexist, and sometimes the use of antipsychotics can break the cycle of escalating hyperarousal and flashbacks.

It may be necessary to take a trauma history many times. In the treatment of complicated cases, it may be necessary to retake the history because initial amnesia or other factors such as shame or apprehension may preclude discussion of certain events and reactions early in treatment. Trauma checklists may be useful in this regard.

The Stage-Oriented Treatment of Trauma

Treatment works, especially when it is made available shortly after the traumatization. Chronicity and comorbidity may complicate responsiveness to treatment. Some trauma victims can tolerate only supportive therapy as reviewing their trauma in detail may be too disruptive. For these patients, accepting the severity of their situations and being with them is the most viable therapeutic stance. As the victim of violence is often in a vulnerable and precarious state, it is important to observe the Hippocratic axiom, "First, do no harm."

There is general consensus that when psychotherapeutic intervention is warranted, it should follow the model of Herman (1992) in which a first stage of safety is followed by a second stage of remembrance and mourning, then by a third stage of reconnection. The stage of safety is designed to help the patient feel safe, understood, protected, and empathized with. It must result in the patient's tolerance of the intimacy in the therapeutic environment (Lindy, 1996). Traumatic material should not be approached until the goals of the safety phase of the treatment, including the establishment of a firm therapeutic alliance, have been achieved. The patient should be willing to approach the material and have rational motivation to do so. In the context of this holding environment, the patient is strengthened and supported and helped to learn and master new coping strategies and methods of symptom containment. In the stage of remembrance and mourning, the patient is helped to tell his or her story, to express feelings associated with and about the trauma and its sequelae, to process the experience in a manner in which it can be integrated with the patient's identity, and to grieve the impact of the trauma and the losses associated with the experience of traumatization on the patient himself or herself, as well as to grieve those who may have been lost or injured in the traumatic event. Despite the controversies associated with traumatic memory and recovered memory, this stage of treatment must address the patient's subjective experience of traumatization. Although it may not be clear that the traumatic material that is presented is historically accurate, and additional material of uncertain veracity may emerge in the course of the therapy, this material communicates the patient's narrative of his or her experience, and it must be addressed. If efforts must be made to lift an amnesia to address some symptoms or problem areas, it is crucial to explain to the patient that any material that may be recovered must be regarded as tentative and of uncertain historical accuracy. Informed consent should be obtained before proceeding with such efforts. It is important to appreciate that in many patients, most traumatic material will never receive either definitive confirmation or disconfirmation. Although many deplore the difficulties and discomforts associated with this stage of therapy, most authorities concur that full recovery is unlikely to occur in its absence. Memories must be processed for continuity of personal identity to be restored and for the patient to make sense of what has befallen him or her. The final stage, reconnection, involves the bringing together of the patient's identity, the reintegration of the patient into his or her social roles and responsibilities, and the resolution of the impacts of the various dysregulations associated with the trauma response. To as great an extent as possible, the patient's sense of having been damaged, demoralized, and made different in a negative and shameful way as a result of the trauma must be mollified and eliminated.

The Orientation of the Treatment

Treatment must be individualized and must accept the unique configuration of strengths, vulnerabilities, comorbidities, values, cultural factors, and existential and spiritual concerns of the patient. Consequently, in treating chronic posttraumatic stress it may be necessary to develop a treatment plan that involves many modalities of treatment in concert. Short-term treatments may prove ineffective, inappropriate, and raise false hopes, which, when dashed, may further complicate the patient's treatment. Although some such therapies may proceed smoothly within a given modality, many treatments come to resemble a series of short-term psychotherapies imbricated within a single long-term psychotherapy. Continuity of care is an important aspect of long-term treatment, and the object constancy and reliability of the therapist may be one of the most important factors in treatment success. When managed care organizations dictate a brief or limited treatment, the psychiatrist should try to address the need for more extensive care with that organization. In treating the patient, it may be necessary to rely more heavily on medication and symptom reduction and have briefer or more spread-out sessions.

Treatment of the victimized patient must be supportive and exploratory although having a here-and-now focus in addition to addressing traumatic material. This combination tests the capacity of the patient and the therapist to collaborate. It is useful to address traumatic material early in the session, reserving the final third of the session for the restabilization of the patient. The status of comorbid conditions should be optimized. The therapist should have the requisite skills, and the logistics of the treatment should be capable of supporting the effort. In unusual circumstances the therapist may conclude that even though a patient is unstable, only work with particular traumatic material will make stabilization possible. When a decision is made to proceed in this manner, it is essential to address only the amount of trauma that must be dealt with before returning to work on stabilization (Kluft, 1997). In a given treatment, the unique situation of the patient, the stage of the treatment, the material under discussion, life circumstances (stressors, crises, and supports), and comorbid conditions will determine how the treatment should be directed. The therapist must be prepared to be flexible and responsive as circumstances change.

In general, trauma patient populations are on a continuum regarding comorbidity and intactness. Some patients are relatively intact and have had little or no comorbidity accompanying their posttraumatic sequelae. The trauma is either recent enough that major characterological changes have not occurred, or if they have, they have not solidified. Such patients are more likely to have, overall, a more exploratory than supportive therapy, unless they recover with a brief period of support. Their difficulties are mostly in connection with the trauma, and the trauma must be a major focus. Another group has considerable comorbidity or some compromise of ego strength or more severity and chronicity of the posttraumatic response or some combination of these. This group may be more depleted or have had less ego strength or both. The treatment course of these patients is likely to be more up and down and more prolonged, with more attention to coping and here-and-now issues, which often prove to have a trauma-based origin. The treatment will alternate between an exploratory and a supportive focus, moving forward with the trauma work at advantageous and stable moments, which Briere (1991) has described as "windows of opportunity." Often the patient will require long periods of work on issues related to comorbid conditions and situational crises. At the end of the continuum is a group that has great severity or chronicity in the trauma response or both, and severe ego weakness or comorbidity or both. Such patients often are destabilized by trauma work. Most of the therapy is directed at efforts to keep the patient stabilized and to coach the patient through the vicissitudes of day-to-day life. There may be occasions in which the traumatic material is briefly addressed, but in general, as soon as it has been dealt with acutely, the focus of treatment returns to a supportive one. With such patients the treatment is palliative and limited in its goals. As therapy progresses, patients in this category may change their characteristics and shift into another category.

It is often helpful to intervene with the trauma victim's family or partner to help concerned others both support and cope with the situation and behaviors of the traumatized person and to address the interpersonal consequences of traumatic sequelae, such as difficulties with intimacy or anger management.

Memory

Many traumatic incidents are recalled very clearly, some are recalled only partially, and some may be absent from available memory for long periods of time. Generally when traumata are recalled, the general nature of the events, gist memory, is well retained, but details may be absent or supplied by a reconstructive process. Most so-called recovered memories of trauma do not take place in or in association with therapy. There is evidence that some recovered memories are inaccurate (called confabulations or pseudomemories), some are rather accurate, and some have mixtures of accurate and inaccurate components. There are no data to indicate what percentage of so-called recovered memories are inaccurate, but there are data to indicate 47 to 95 percent of recovered memories of conventional child abuse are confirmed, and only 1 to 3 percent of bizarre abuse memories are confirmed (Bowman, 1996a, 1996b). A recent study demonstrated that 74 percent of always recalled and 74 percent of recovered memories could be confirmed (Dahlenberg, 1996). No characteristics of memories, such as being clear, emotional, detailed, or held with conviction, are definitively associated with veracity.

Accordingly, considerable controversy surrounds the impact of trauma on memory, the accuracy of memories of trauma, and the accuracy of memories of trauma that enter awareness after a period of amnesia (International Society for Traumatic Stress Studies, 1998). Despite this fact, because dissociative disorders are usually associated with trauma, the issue of memory must be addressed. Notwithstanding the difficulties associated with autobiographical memory, especially when elements of memory are recovered, most authorities concur that unless memories are processed it is difficult to bring about a full recovery in which continuity of personal identity is restored and the patient is able to make sense of what has befallen him or her. As treatment begins, the patient's accounts of his or her circumstances should be heard with empathy and respect. It is not appropriate to begin treatment with efforts to document or disconfirm the patient's allegations of traumatization, although a decision may be made to do so if it is the patient's wish to do so. It is not appropriate to assume that other sources' disagreement with the patient's given history invalidate it, especially if these other sources might be culpable. Therefore, this therapeutic work is pursued, but appropriate cautions about memory issues (acknowledging both the importance of work with autobiographical memories of trauma in the treatment of trauma and the difficulties that may be encountered in work with human memory) are provided to the patient, whose treatment occurs under the aegis of documented informed consent. It is not appropriate for the therapist either to assume that an allegation of trauma is true or false) or that all continuously held memories are accurate and all memories returning to awareness or emerging in the course of therapy are false. Clinicians should be aware that the only proof of the accuracy or inaccuracy of a memory is reliable corroboration by external evidence or witnesses other than alleged abusers. Without corroboration, legal action on the basis of memories that emerge in the course of therapy is usually contraindicated.

The Stance of the Therapist

The stance of the therapist should be warm, friendly, and engaging toward the patient, who may feel damaged, shamed, guilty, and defective. The therapist must have firm boundaries without being punitive or rejecting. Many victims experience boundary violations, however trivial, as hints that the treatment situation is dangerous and that the therapist cannot be trusted. Trauma treatment can be painful in itself and must be conducted in a carefully paced manner that respects the strengths and vulnerabilities of the patient and preserves and enhances function as much as possible.

The trauma victim must be treated in a way that is sensitive to and respectful of the culture, cultural signifiers, and cultural values of the victim and the victim's family. It is vitally important that the therapy be conducted in a manner that does not estrange the victim from his or her family and community on these grounds. Notwithstanding the availability of effective trauma treatments, their application with certain groups may have an unacceptable cost-benefit ratio and may prove either unsuccessful or deleterious. For example, in some Southeast Asian populations, contrary to the case for North Americans and Europeans, it may be contraindicated to attempt to identify and process traumatic experiences (Kinzie, forthcoming).

As in any form of psychotherapeutic intervention, the stance of the therapist in relation to the patient is critical in determining outcome (Blank, 1994). The clinician must be someone who understands posttraumatic syndromes as related initially to external events that are then worked upon by the particular dynamics, fantasies, experience, and meaning-making of the individual patient. Any therapist who hopes to be successful in the treatment of complicated trauma-based syndromes must be willing to develop an understanding of repression, dissociation, isolation of affect, amnesia for parts of events, disguised traumatic dreams, holding of traumatic memories, conflicts and impacted affects in the unconscious over time, symbolic expression of anxiety, and identification with the aggressor (Blank, 1994). Therapists must recognize that by definition, trauma is a boundary violation; therefore, violated patients may have no concept of normal boundary formation or maintenance (Kluft, 1993). It will therefore be the responsibility of the therapist to define and protect boundaries within the therapeutic context. This may necessitate early and open discussion of the therapeutic frame, including length and time of sessions, fee and payment arrangements, the use of health insurance, confidentiality and its limits, therapist availability between sessions, procedure if hospitalization is necessary, patient charts and who has access to them, the use (or nonuse) of physical contact with the therapist, involvement of the patient's family or significant others in the treatment, discussion of the therapist's expectations concerning management by the patient of self-destructive behavior, legal ramifications of the use of hypnosis as part of the treatment (material recalled in trance is not likely to be admissible evidence in any legal action undertaken by the patient), among others (International Society for the Study of Dissociation, 1997).

Trauma survivors are often driven to unconsciously and nonverbally reenact their experiences within the context of close relationships. This traumatic reenactment may drive the therapeutic relationship to destruction if it is not properly understood, analyzed, and transmuted. Even experienced clinicians may find themselves unwittingly drawn into scenarios in which they are alternately playing out the roles of helpless victim, powerless rescuer, or malicious perpetrator. The management of such complex, nonverbal enactment often necessitates ongoing consultation with trusted colleagues in the form of individual or group supervision and can play a vital role in helping the therapist maintain balance and the safety of the therapeutic alliance (Bloom, 1997).

The treatment of the traumatized has the potential to make a strong impact upon the therapist. The clinician who works with traumatized individuals must make efforts to monitor his or her countertransference and to monitor him or herself for secondary or vicarious posttraumatic stress, also referred to as "compassion fatigue" (Figley, 1995a, 1995b), "vicarious traumatization" (McCann and Pearlman, 1990; Pearlman, 1995; Pearlman and Saakvitne, 1995), and "covictimization" (Hartsough and Myers, 1985). People who are repeatedly exposed to the effects of violence, even though only secondarily, can be traumatized themselves and even experience symptoms similar to victims of posttraumatic stress. It is somewhat different from burnout, which is a state of physical, emotional, and mental exhaustion caused by the long-term involvement in very emotionally draining situations (Pines and Arenson, 1988). Burnout emerges gradually, whereas secondary traumatic stress can emerge suddenly and without much warning, often accompanied by a sense of confusion and helplessness (Figley, 1995a, 1995b). In such cases, exposure to a traumatizing event experienced by one person becomes a traumatizing event for the second person. The hallmark of vicarious traumatization is a disrupted frame of reference. Repeated exposure to man-made violence can impact on our willingness and ability to relate to others and on how we make sense of a frightening world. As a result of exposure to victims of violence, clinicians may experience disruptions in their sense of identity, world view, and spirituality that may interfere dramatically with treatment if not addressed in some way, often through peer supervision (Pearlman, 1995; Pearlman and Saakvitne, 1995).

The Principles of Good Trauma Therapy

Traumatized persons with posttraumatic conditions have become "stuck" on the trauma and its sequelae. The treatment aims "to help them move from being haunted by the past and interpreting subsequent emotionally arousing stimuli as a return of the trauma, to being fully engaged in the present and becoming capable of responding to current exigencies" (van der Kolk, McFarlane, and van der Hart, 1996, p. 419). They must regain control over their emotional responses and place the trauma in perspective as a historical event or events that can be expected not to recur if they take charge of their lives. They must come to integrate what has occurred, however ego-alien, unacceptable, terrifying, and incomprehensible into their self-concepts. They must make these elements integrated rather than dissociated so they are no longer intrusive and destabilizing. Their anxieties must be deconditioned, and they must change their views of themselves and the world by establishing a sense of personal integrity and control (van der Kolk, 1996b). Typically, intrusive experiencing, autonomic hyperarousal, avoidant and numbing strategies, emotional dysregulation, difficulties with learning and mastery, problems with amnesia and dissociation, aggression toward self and others, and somatization will have to be addressed.

Kluft (1996a) put forward several principles for the therapist who deals with the traumatized: As trauma involves the breaking of boundaries, an effective trauma treatment will have a secure treatment frame and firm consistent boundaries. As trauma imposes dyscontrol and helplessness, a successful treatment will focus on mastery and the patient's active participation in the treatment process. As trauma is imposed involuntarily, a successful trauma therapy will build and maintain a strong therapeutic alliance. As trauma leads to dissociation and a failure to integrate experience into memory and identity, what has been hidden away must be returned to awareness, and associated emotional responses verbalized with feeling. As trauma often leads to dissociated alternate perceptions or narratives of life events, there must be clear communication and efforts to integrate disparate perceptions. As trauma often results in the shattering of basic assumptions (invulnerability, meaning, and self-esteem), efforts must be made to restore morale and to inculcate realistic hope. As trauma overwhelms a patient's resources and supports, treatment must be carefully paced to minimize avoidable overwhelming experiences and aggressively address issues of hyperarousal. As trauma often is related to the irresponsibility of important others, the therapist must model, teach, and reinforce responsibility. As trauma usually induces shame, the therapist must take an active, warm, and flexible stance that emphasizes empathic connectedness with the patient. As trauma often interferes with learning and cognition, therapy must address and attempt to correct defective cognition and work strenuously to help the patient find words that match his or her experiences.

Because the target symptoms may be numerous and involve all manner of biopsychosocial matters, eclecticism and the collaboration with other colleagues who may have contributions to make to the treatment are essential. For example, dissociative disorders usually require specific treatments in order to achieve resolution. Whether a dissociative disorder is the main manifestation of the trauma response or a comorbid condition, the therapist should be prepared to either provide specific treatment or to collaborate with a colleague who can provide this element of the psychotherapy.

It is important to appreciate that these principles apply to all treatment modalities and across all treatment settings. Hospital units that address the treatment of the traumatized must model these goals, attitudes, and principles if they are to participate meaningfully in the continuum of care for trauma patients.

Hospitalizing the Traumatized Patient

The inpatient milieu treatment of these patients deserves special mention as their rate of hospitalization can be quite high. Likewise, on any general psychiatric inpatient unit, a significant proportion of the population will have experienced a history of traumatic events that may be playing an important and unrecognized role in the development and maintenance of their psychiatric symptoms. Bloom (1997) has written about the implications of what is described above as "good trauma therapy" for the short-term inpatient unit.

The indications for hospitalization of the trauma patient include

Suicidality or homicidality

Psychosis

Affective instability or deterioration of a mood disorder to the point that function is impaired

A significant problem with the outpatient treatment team or dynamic that places the patient at risk (for example, the therapist is in trouble)

Need for diagnostic clarification (psychotic disorder versus dissociative disorder versus medical problem or some combination of these)

Significant reenactment behaviors that are interfering significantly with home, work, parenting, or relationships and are not responding to usual outpatient interventions

Other self-destructive behavior that is escalating and increasingly out of the patient's ability to control

Serious threat to the patient's life and well-being secondary to a violent relationship

Patients who end up hospitalized often suffer from very complex clinical pictures and therefore benefit enormously from the power of a team approach to evaluation and treatment. The purpose of hospitalization is to build a better outpatient (Kluft, 1996b), and this is effectively accomplished by mobilizing a group of people to look simultaneously at various aspects of the problem, including medical ones. Because of short hospital stays, treatment planning must be well organized and supervised. Goals must be clearly defined and limited to what is attainable during a brief stay. Usually, the major goal is the achievement of safety with self and others, and the patient must be an active agent in all treatment decisions. As much as possible, nothing should be done that encourages further helplessness and regression. All interventions must be directed toward the empowerment of the patient in restoration of self-control. Everyone in the milieu must maintain clear and well-defined boundaries and expectations while providing an environment that is open to the construction of a narrative that helps put the traumatic experience into perspective. The safety of the inpatient unit is necessary as memories of the past flood into consciousness, producing overwhelming hyperarousal and unmodulated affect. The restoration of memories should be encouraged only if the patient has demonstrated sufficient capacity for safety that regression will not occur (Bloom, 1997).

The power of the therapeutic community, even in a short-term unit, should be drawn upon to help patients mobilize their own internal resources and draw on the strengths of others. Extensive efforts should be made to educate everyone in the milieu, usually through psychoeducational groups, about the effects of trauma, the responsible use of medications, the hazards of self-destructive coping skills, and the need for withdrawal from self-medication, self-mutilation, and other forms of destructive attempts at affect management.

Given the fact that these patients frequently need much more time in a protective environment than they receive, it should come as no surprise that there is a high rate of recidivism in this population. Good communication between inpatient and outpatient therapists can at least make necessary transitions as positive as possible, despite the current, often extreme, limitations of the system.

Modalities of Treatment

Traumatized individuals may manifest extremely complex presentations accompanied by considerable morbidity that changes over time. It is essential to individualize psychotherapy and to anticipate using different modalities over the course of the treatment. Because additional modalities provided by additional therapists may prove essential to the treatment, it becomes essential for the primary therapist to maintain rapport with the patient even when many parties may play a role in the treatment and even though the application of some additional modalities may temporarily interrupt work with the primary therapist. The socializing of the patient to the therapy and the discussion of the therapeutic alliance should address from the first the possibility of involving additional mental health professionals as the treatment proceeds.

Although cognitive-behavioral techniques have been researched most thoroughly, many specialized approaches to trauma are currently being developed and applied. Hypnosis has a venerable history in the treatment of trauma and remains a useful tool not withstanding controversy about its impact on memory. Eye movement desensitization and reprocessing is gaining popularity and appears quite useful. Single-modality approaches have been most successful for single-adult traumata. However, with patients exposed to extensive childhood trauma, trauma has not only had its usual consequences, it often has interrupted developmental processes. When dissociative psychopathology is a significant aspect of the posttraumatic symptomatology, approaches specific to the resolution of dissociative difficulties should be introduced. In addition to a basic individual psychotherapy and other technique-oriented individual interventions, ancillary approaches such as group psychotherapy, art therapy, movement therapy, music therapy, and body-oriented treatments may play a valuable role for selected patients. Treatment should begin as rapidly as possible to prevent both psychobiological consequences and demoralization.

Symptom reduction is extremely important both to treat posttraumatic and comorbid conditions and to stabilize the patient sufficiently to proceed to and manage the stage of remembrance and mourning. In this regard medication may play a valuable role. Symptom reduction, especially for intrusive symptoms and sleep difficulties, may also facilitate the engagement of the patient in therapy.

Psychopharmacology

There is no definitive psychopharmacological treatment for trauma-related symptoms. This is understandable given that so many different neurobiological systems seem to be involved in posttraumatic disorders. So far, it appears that at least PTSD is associated with abnormalities in the adrenergic, hypothalamic-pituitary-adrenocortical, opioid, dopaminergic, and thyroid systems, and possibly with alternations in the serotonergic, gamma amino buteric acid benzodiazepine and the N-methyl-D-aspartate systems (Friedman and Southwick, 1995). Medications may help some of the symptoms of posttraumatic stress; they are much more successful in alleviating depression, sleep disorders, anxiety, and hyperarousal symptoms than in helping withdrawal and numbing. To complicate matters, many patients with trauma-related syndromes use a variety of substances in an effort at self-medication. Among treatment-seeking patients, from 60 percent to 80 percent suffer from alcohol or drug abuse or dependence. There are relatively few controlled, double-blind studies of the efficacy of medications in these disorders, and those that have been done have largely been tried on combat veterans.

Drug therapy has been suggested by van der Kolk (1996a) based on the major biological models for PTSD. Adrenergic dysregulation suggests that the use of antidepressants of all groups (monoamine oxidase [MAO] inhibitors and tricyclic antidepressants) may be helpful. Other drugs such as clonidine, an alpha 1 agonist that reduces hyperarousal symptoms and nightmares by reducing central nervous system norepinephrine, may also be used (Porter and Bell, 1999). Furthermore, many dissociative patients often do well with clonazepam or other benzodiazepines. It is important not to misdiagnose dissociative phenomenology as psychosis and initiate a regimen that will not lead to the resolution of the dissociative symptomatology. Beta-adrenergic blockers might also be used for adrenergic dysregulation. Serotonergic dysfunction suggests the use of serotonergic drugs such as selective serotonin reuptake inhibitors (SSRIs), which has been supported by recent clinical trials. The kindling hypotheses for traumatic stress suggests the use of anti-kindling drugs such as carbamazepine. Finally, the increased startle responsiveness suggests the possibility that clonazepam and buspirone may be effective. In selected patients a wide variety of medications and many combinations of medications can prove useful.

According to these authors, the purposes of medication in PTSD are as follows:

Reduction of frequency or severity of intrusive symptoms
Reduction of the tendency to interpret incoming stimuli as recurrences of the trauma
Reduction of conditioned hyperarousal to stimuli reminiscent of the trauma, as well as in generalized hyperarousal
Reduction of avoidance behavior
Reduction of depressed mood and numbing
Reduction of psychotic or dissociative symptoms
Reduction of impulsive aggression against self and others

In view of the myriad psychobiological lesions associated with trauma, it is not surprising that polypharmacy is usually necessary to achieve maximal symptom reduction.

In practice, it is important to remember that no drug cures trauma and that medication is generally directed at the treatment of depression, anxiety, obsessions, compulsions, and psychosis—all of which can coexist with, or be a part of, trauma-related syndromes (Bell, 1997). The symptom relief often enables the person to move ahead in therapy and achieve a higher degree of function when used in concert with other forms of treatment. It is especially crucial that the psychiatrist avoid both the Scylla and Charybdis of the psychopharmacology of the traumatized: either undermedicating a seriously distressed patient or trying to make the medication a substitute for an appropriate trauma-resolving psychotherapy.

Recommendations

Mental health professionals (MHPs) should promote awareness of trauma as a biopsychosocial phenomenon important in the development of psychopathology, contributing to increased comorbidity for both mental and physical disorders, and responsible for enormous economic costs to society.

Accordingly, the mental health profession should advocate for education about trauma, trauma-related disorders, and the treatment of the consequences of trauma in training. In addition, MHPs should advocate for insurance to provide trauma victims with access for care adequate to their needs, which are often long term. Psychiatrists should support the systematic assessment of patients for histories of trauma, for trauma-related disorders, and for the sequelae of trauma as part of routine psychiatric, medical, and medical emergency assessment. This includes encouraging psychiatrists in practice to obtain up-to-date knowledge about trauma, its consequences, and its treatment. Finally, MHPs should support both clinical assessments and research that study the impact of trauma on the individual, family, and community and study factors associated with vulnerability to trauma and with resilience to trauma. This includes advocating the increasingly robust science of memory as it is relevant to the treatment of the traumatized by showing that the polarized positions on recovered memory—that recovered memories are either inherently reliable or inherently unreliable—are inconsistent with established data.

References

American Medical Association. *Diagnostic and Treatment Guidelines on Domestic Violence.* Chicago: American Medical Association, 1992.

American Psychiatric Association. *Diagnostic and Statistical Manual of Mental Disorders: Fourth Edition.* Washington, D.C.: American Psychiatric Press, 1994.

Amir, M., and others. "Post-Traumatic Stress Disorder, Tenderness and Fibromyalgia." *Journal of Psychosomatic Research,* 1997, *42*(6), 607–613.

Anfuso, D. "Deflecting Workplace Violence." *Personnel Journal,* 1994, *73*(10), 66–78.

Angst, J., Degonda, M., and Ernst, C. "The Zurich Study. XV: Suicide Attempts in a Cohort from Age 20 to 30." *European Archives of Psychiatry and Clinical Neuroscience,* 1992, *242*(2–3), 135–141.

Badura, A. S., Reiter, R. C., Altmaier, E. M., and Rhomberg, A. "Dissociation, Somatization, Substance Abuse, and Coping in Women with Chronic Pelvic Pain." *Obstetrics and Gynecology,* 1997, *90*(3), 405–410.

Bell, C. C. "Stress-Related Disorders in African-American Children." *Journal of the National Medical Association,* 1997, *89*(5), 335–340.

Bell, C. C., Taylor-Crawford, K., Jenkins, E. J., and Chalmers, D. "Need for Victimization Screening in a Black Psychiatric Population." *Journal of the National Medical Association,* 1988, *80*(1), 41–48.

Benedikt, R. A., and Kolb, L. C. "Preliminary Findings on Chronic Pain and Post-Traumatic Stress Disorder." *American Journal of Psychiatry,* 1986, *143*(7), 908–910.

Blank, A. S. "Clinical Detection, Diagnosis, and Differential Diagnosis of Post-Traumatic Stress Disorder." *Psychiatric Clinics of North America,* 1994, *17*(2), 351–383.

Bloom, S. L. *Creating Sanctuary: Toward the Evolution of Sane Societies.* New York: Routledge, 1997.

Bowman, E. S. "Delayed Memories of Child Abuse. Part I: An Overview of Research Findings on Forgetting, Remembering, and Corroborating Trauma." *Dissociation,* 1996a, *9,* 221–230.

Bowman, E. S. "Delayed Memories of Child Abuse. Part II: An Overview of Research Findings Relevant to Understanding Their Reliability and Suggestibility." *Dissociation,* 1996b, *9,* 231–240.

Breslau, N., Davis, G. C., Andreski, P., and Peterson, E. "Traumatic Events and Post-traumatic Stress Disorder in an Urban Population of Young Adults." *Archives of General Psychiatry*, 1991, *48*, 216–222.

Briere, J. *Treating Victims of Child Sexual Abuse*. San Francisco: Jossey-Bass, 1991.

Bushnell, J. A., Wells, J. E., and Oakley-Browne, M. A. "Long-Term Effects of Intrafamilial Sexual Abuse in Childhood." *Acta Psychiatrica Scandinavia*, 1992, *85*(2), 136–142.

Connors, M. E., and Morse, W. "Sexual Abuse and Eating Disorders: A Review." *International Journal of Eating Disorders*, 1993, *13*(1), 1–11.

Dahlenberg, C. J. "Accuracy, Timing, and Circumstances of Disclosure in Therapy of Recovered and Continuous Memories of Abuse." *The Journal of Psychiatry and the Law*, 1996, *24*, 229–275.

Davidson, J.R.T., Hughes, D., Blazer, D. and George, L. K. "Post-Traumatic Stress Disorder in the Community: An Epidemiological Study." *Psychological Medicine*, 1991, *21*, 713–721.

Drossman, D. A. "Sexual and Physical Abuse and Gastrointestinal Illness." *Scandinavian Journal of Gastroenterology*, 1995, *208*(supplement), 90–96.

Ellason, J. W., Ross, C. A., Sainton, K., and Mayran, L. W. "Axis I and II Comorbidity and Childhood Trauma History in Chemical Dependency." *Bulletin of the Menninger Clinic*, 1996, *60*(1), 39–51.

Figley, C. R. *Compassion Fatigue: Coping with Secondary Traumatic Stress Disorder in Those Who Treat the Traumatized*. New York: Brunner/Mazel, 1995a.

Figley, C. R. "Compassion Fatigue: Toward a New Understanding of the Costs of Caring." In B. H. Stamm (ed.), *Secondary Traumatic Stress: Self-Care Issues for Clinicians, Researchers, and Educators*. Lutherville, Md.: Sidran, 1995b.

Friedman, M. J., and Southwick, S. M. "Toward Pharmacotherapy for Post-Traumatic Stress Disorder." In M. J. Friedman, D. S. Charney, and A. Y. Deutch (eds.), *Neurobiological and Clinical Consequences of Stress: From Normal Adaptation to PTSD*. Philadelphia: Lippincott-Raven, 1995.

Fukudo, S., Nomura, T., Muranaka, M., and Taguchi, F. "Brain-Gut Response to Stress and Cholinergic Stimulation in Irritable Bowel Syndrome: A Preliminary Study." *Journal of Clinical Gastroenterology*, 1993, *17*(2), 133–141.

Geisser, M. E., Roth, R. S., Bachman, J. E., and Eckert, T. A. "The Relationship Between Symptoms of Post-Traumatic Stress Disorder and Pain, Affective Disturbance, and Disability Among Patients with Accident- and Nonaccident-Related Pain." *Pain*, 1996, *66*(2-3), 207–214.

Grady, K. T. "Posttraumatic Stress Disorder and Comorbidity: Recognizing the Many Faces of PTSD." *Journal of Clinical Psychiatry*, 1997, *58*(supplement 9), 12–15.

Hartsough, D., and Myers, D. *Disaster Work and Mental Health: Prevention and Control of Stress Among Workers*. Washington, D.C.: National Institute of Mental Health, Center for Mental Health Studies of Emergencies, 1985.

Herman, J. L. *Trauma and Recovery*. New York: Basic Books, 1992.

Herman, J. L., Perry, J. C., and van der Kolk, B. A. "Childhood Trauma in Borderline Personality Disorder." *American Journal of Psychiatry*, 1989, *146*, 490–495.

International Society for the Study of Dissociation. *Guidelines for Treating Dissociative Identity Disorder*. Glenview, Ill.: International Society for the Study of Dissociation, 1997.

International Society for Traumatic Stress Studies. *Childhood Trauma Remembered: A Report on the Current Scientific Knowledge Base and Its Application*. Northbrook, Ill.: International Society for Traumatic Stress Studies, 1998.

Irwin, C., and others. "Comorbidity of Posttraumatic Stress Disorder and Irritable Bowel Syndrome." *Journal of Clinical Psychiatry*, 1996, *57*(12), 576–578.

Jenkins, E. J., and Bell, C. C. "Exposure and Response to Community Violence Among Children and Adolescents." In J. Osofsky (ed.), *Children in a Violent Society*. New York: Guilford Press, 1997.

Jenkins, E., Bell, C. C., Taylor, J., and Walker, L. "Circumstances of Sexual and Physical Victimization of Black Psychiatric Outpatients." *Journal of the National Medical Association,* 1989, *81*(3), 246–252.

Kessler, R., and others. "Posttraumatic Stress Disorder in the National Comorbidity Survey." *Archives of General Psychiatry,* 1995, *52,* 1048–1060.

Kinzie, J. D. "Cross-Cultural Treatment of PTSD." In J. P. Wilson, M. J. Friedman, and J. Lindy (eds.), *Core Approaches for the Treatment of PTSD.* New York: Guilford Press, forthcoming.

Kinzie, J. D., and Boehnlein, J. K. "Psychotherapy of Victims of Massive Violence." *American Journal of Psychotherapy,* 1993, *47,* 90–102.

Kluft, R. P. "Basic Principles in Conducting the Psychotherapy of Multiple Personality Disorder." In R. P. Kluft and C. G. Fine (eds.), *Clinical Perspectives on Multiple Personality Disorder.* Washington, D.C.: American Psychiatric Press, 1993.

Kluft, R. P. "Dissociative Identity Disorder." In G. O. Gabbard (ed.), *Treatments of Psychiatric Disorders.* Washington, D.C.: American Psychiatric Press, 1996a.

Kluft, R. P. "Hospital Treatment." In J. L. Spira (ed.), *Treating Dissociative Identity Disorder.* San Francisco: Jossey-Bass, 1996b.

Kluft, R. P. "On the Treatment of the Traumatic Memories of DID Patients: Always? Never? Sometimes? Now? Later?" *Dissociation,* 1997, *10,* 80–90.

Koss, M. P., Koss, P. G., and Woodruff, W. J. "Deleterious Effects of Criminal Victimization on Women's Health and Medical Utilization." *Archives of Internal Medicine,* 1991, *151*(2), 342–347.

Leserman, J., and others. "Sexual and Physical Abuse History in Gastroenterology Practice: How Types of Abuse Impact Health Status." *Psychosomatic Medicine,* 1996, *58*(1), 4–15.

Leserman, J., Toomey, T. C., and Drossman, D. A. "Medical Consequences of Sexual and Physical Abuse in Women." *Humane Medicine,* 1995, *11*(1), 23–28.

Lindy, J. D. "Psychoanalytic Psychotherapy of Posttraumatic Stress Disorder: The Nature of the Therapeutic Relationship." In B. A. van der Kolk, A. C. McFarlane, and L. Weisaeth (eds.), *Traumatic Stress: The Effects of Overwhelming Experience on Mind, Body, and Society.* New York: Guilford Press, 1996.

McCann, I. L., and Pearlman, L. A. "Vicarious Traumatization: A Framework for Understanding the Psychological Effects of Working with Victims." *Journal of Traumatic Stress,* 1990, *3,* 131–147.

Miller, T. R., and Cohen, M. A. "Costs of Gunshot and Cut/Stab Wounds in the United States, with Some Canadian Comparisons." *Accident Analysis and Prevention,* 1997, *29*(3), 329–341.

Miller, T. R., Cohen, M. A., and Rossman, S. B. "Victim Costs of Violent Crime and Resulting Injuries." *Health Affairs,* 1993, *12*(4), 186–197.

Miller, T. R., Cohen, M., and Wiersema, B. *Victim Costs and Consequences: A New Look.* Washington, D.C.: U.S. Department of Justice, National Institute of Justice, 1996.

National Victim Center. *Crime and Victimization in America: Statistical Overview.* Arlington, Va.: National Victim Center, 1993.

Norris, F. H. "Epidemiology of Trauma: Frequency and Impact of Different Potentially Traumatic Events on Different Demographic Groups." *Journal of Consulting and Clinical Psychology,* 1992, *60,* 409–418.

Pearlman, L. A. "Self-Care for Trauma Therapists: Ameliorating Vicarious Traumatization." In B. H. Stamm (ed.), *Secondary Traumatic Stress: Self-Care Issues for Clinicians, Researchers, and Educators.* Lutherville, Md.: Sidran, 1995.

Pearlman, L. A., and Saakvitne, K. W. *Trauma and the Therapist: Countertransference and Vicarious Traumatization in Psychotherapy with Incest Survivors.* New York: Norton, 1995.

Pecukonis, E. V. "Childhood Sex Abuse in Women with Chronic Intractable Back Pain." *Social Work and Health Care,* 1996, *23*(3), 1–16.

Perry, J. C., Herman, J. L., van der Kolk, B. A., and Hoke, L. A. "Psychotherapy and Psychological Trauma in Borderline Personality Disorder." *Psychiatric Annals*, 1990, *20*, 33–43.

Pines, A. M., and Arenson, E. *Career Burnout: Causes and Cures.* New York: Free Press, 1988.

Plichta, S. B., and Abraham, C. "Violence and Gynecologic Health in Women More Than 50 Years Old." *American Journal of Obstetrics and Gynecology*, 1996, *174*(3), 903–907.

Pollack, M. H., Otto, M. W., Rosenbaum, J. F., and Sachs, G. S. "Personality Disorders in Patients with Panic Disorder: Association with Childhood Anxiety Disorders, Early Trauma, Comorbidity, and Chronicity." *Comprehensive Psychiatry*, 1992, *33*(2), 78–83.

Porter, D. M, and Bell, C. C. "The Use of Clonidine in Post-Traumatic Stress Disorder." *Journal of the National Medical Association*, 1999, *91*, 475–477.

Resnick, H., and others. "Prevalence of Civilian Trauma and Posttraumatic Stress Disorder in a Representative National Sample of Women." *Journal of Consulting and Clinical Psychology*, 1993, *61*, 984–991.

Salmon, P., and Calderbank, S. "The Relationship of Childhood Physical and Sexual Abuse to Adult Illness Behavior." *Journal of Psychosomatic Research*, 1996, *40* (3), 329–336.

Shalev, A. Y. "Stress Versus Traumatic Stress: From Acute Homeostatic Reactions to Chronic Psychopathology." In B. A. van der Kolk, A. C. McFarlane, and L. Weisaeth (eds.), *Traumatic Stress: The Effects of Overwhelming Experience on Mind, Body, and Society.* New York: Guilford Press, 1996.

Silver, S. M. "An Inpatient Program for Post-Traumatic Stress Disorder: Context as Treatment." In C. R. Figley (ed.), *Trauma and Its Wake.* Vol. 2: *Post-Traumatic Stress Disorder: Theory, Research, and Treatment.* New York: Brunner/Mazel, 1986.

Solomon, S. D., and Davidson, J.R.T. "Trauma: Prevalence, Impairment, Service Use, and Cost." *Journal of Clinical Psychiatry*, 1997, *58*(supplement 9), 5–11.

Southwick, S. M., Yehuda, R., and Giller, E. L. "Personality Disorders in Treatment-Seeking Combat Veterans with Posttraumatic Stress Disorder." *American Journal of Psychiatry*, 1993, *150*, 1020–1023.

U.S. Department of Health and Human Services. *The Third National Incidence Study of Child Abuse and Neglect.* Washington, D.C.: U.S. GPO, 1996.

van der Kolk, B. A. "The Compulsion to Repeat the Trauma: Re-enactment, Re-victimization, and Masochism." *Psychiatric Clinics of North America*, 1989, *12*, 389–411.

van der Kolk, B. A. "The Body Keeps the Score: Approaches to the Psychobiology of Posttraumatic Stress Disorder." In B. A. van der Kolk, A. C. McFarlane, and L. Weisaeth (eds.), *Traumatic Stress: The Effects of Overwhelming Experience on Mind, Body, and Society.* New York: Guilford Press, 1996a.

van der Kolk, B. A. "The Complexity of Adaptation to Trauma: Self-Regulation, Stimulus Discrimination, and Characterological Development." In B. A. van der Kolk, A. C. McFarlane, and L. Weisaeth (eds.), *Traumatic Stress: The Effects of Overwhelming Experience on Mind, Body, and Society.* New York: Guilford Press, 1996b.

van der Kolk, B. A., McFarlane, A. C., and van der Hart, O. "A General Approach to Treatment of Posttraumatic Stress Disorder." In B. A. van der Kolk, A. C. McFarlane, and L. Weisaeth (eds.), *Traumatic Stress: The Effects of Overwhelming Experience on Mind, Body, and Society.* New York: Guilford Press, 1996.

van der Kolk, B. A., McFarlane, A. C., and Weisaeth, L. (eds.). *Traumatic Stress: The Effects of Overwhelming Experience on Mind, Body, and Society.* New York: Guilford Press, 1996.

Walinsky, A. "The Crisis of Public Order." *Atlantic Monthly,* July 1995, pp. 39–54.

Walker, E. A., and others. "Medical and Psychiatric Symptoms in Women with Childhood Sexual Abuse." *Psychosomatic Medicine,* 1992, *54*(6), 658–664.

Walker, E. A., and others. "Chronic Pelvic Pain and Gynecological Symptoms in Women with Irritable Bowel Syndrome." *Journal of Psychosomatic Obstetrics and Gynecology,* 1996, *17*(1), 39–46.

Walling, M. K., and others. "Abuse History and Chronic Pain in Women. II: A Multivariate Analysis of Abuse and Psychological Morbidity." *Obstetrics and Gynecology,* 1994, *84*(2), 200–206.

Yarborough, M. H. "Securing the American Workplace." *HR Focus,* 1994, *71*(9), 1–4.

RICHARD P. KLUFT *is clinical professor of psychiatry at Temple University School of Medicine and is in the private practice of psychiatry and psychoanalysis in Bala Cynwyd, Pennsylvania.*

SANDRA L. BLOOM *is executive director of the Sanctuary Programs at Horsham Clinic, Ambler, Pennsylvania, and Hampton Hospital, Rancocas, New Jersey, and author of* Creating Sanctuary: Toward the Evolution of Sane Societies.

J. DAVID KINZIE *is professor of psychiatry at Oregon Health Sciences University in Portland.*

INDEX

Back Issue/Subscription Order Form

Copy or detach and send to:
Jossey-Bass Inc., 350 Sansome Street, San Francisco CA 94104-1342

Call or fax toll free!
Phone 888-378-2537 6AM–5PM PST; Fax 800-605-2665

Back issues: Please send me the following issues at $25 each.
(Important: please include series initials and issue number, such as MHS81.)

1.MHS _____

_____

_____

$ _____ Total for single issues

$ _____ Shipping charges (for single issues *only;* subscriptions are exempt
from shipping charges): Up to $30, add $5^{50} • $30^{01}–$50, add $6^{50}
$50^{01}–$75, add $7^{50} • $75^{01}–$100, add $9 • $100^{01}–$150, add $10
Over $150, call for shipping charge.

Subscriptions   Please ❑ start   ❑ renew my subscription to *New Directions for Mental Health Services* for the year_____ at the following rate:

     ❑ Individual $65   ❑ Institutional $110
NOTE: Subscriptions are quarterly, and are for the calendar year only.
Subscriptions begin with the spring issue of the year indicated above.
For shipping outside the U.S., please add $25.

$ _____ Total single issues and subscriptions (CA, IN, NJ, NY, and DC
residents, add sales tax for single issues. NY and DC residents must
include shipping charges when calculating sales tax. NY and Canadian
residents only, add sales tax for subscriptions.)

❑ Payment enclosed (U.S. check or money order only)

❑ VISA, MC, AmEx, Discover Card #_____ Exp. date_____

Signature _____ Day phone _____

❑ Bill me (U.S. institutional orders only. Purchase order required.)

Purchase order #_____

Name _____

Address _____

_____

_____

Phone_____ E-mail _____

For more information about Jossey-Bass, visit our Web site at:
www.josseybass.com   **PRIORITY CODE = ND1**

OTHER TITLES AVAILABLE IN THE NEW DIRECTIONS FOR MENTAL HEALTH
SERVICES SERIES
H. Richard Lamb, Editor-in-Chief